RACQUETBALL

about the authors

Dr. Philip E. Allsen, currently a professor of Physical Education at Brigham Young University, has been active in many aspects of physical education. He earned his B.S. at Ricks College, M.S. at Brigham Young University, and Ed.D. at the University of Utah. He has held positions at all three schools and has also served as athletic director for the city of Gardena, California, and as a Physical Fitness Officer in the U.S. Navy. Dr. Allsen has held his present position for the past 14 years. He holds honors and memberships in many professional organizations, ranging from the American College of Sports Medicine to the Nutrition Today Society. He is the author of over 60 professional articles. Besides co-authoring three editions of *Racquetball* for WCB, Dr. Allsen has also helped author three other books published by WCB; *Fitness For Life, Physical Fitness and Conditioning: Current Answers to Relevant Questions,* and *Jogging.*

Professor Alan R. (Pete) Witbeck has been involved in racquetball as a teacher and outstanding player for the past 20 years and continues to teach three sections of racquetball each semester. Professor Witbeck, who took both his B.S. and M.S. degrees at Brigham Young University, has been a member of the faculty there for 25 years, presently serving as Assistant Athletic Director. He has also compiled a successful coaching record at BYU. During 5 years as freshman basketball coach, his teams had an overall record of 62 wins and 9 losses, including one undefeated season, and during the first 10 years of the Western Athletic Conference, as varsity assistant, the BYU team won 5 championships.

Both authors are firm believers in physical conditioning for all ages and enjoy many sports besides racquetball.

RACQUETBALL

Third Edition

Physical Education Activities Series

Philip E. Allsen
Brigham Young University

Pete Witbeck
Brigham Young University

wcb
Wm C Brown Company Publishers
Dubuque, Iowa

Consulting Editors

Physical Education
Aileene Lockhart
Texas Woman's University

Parks and Recreation
David Gray
California State University, Long Beach

Health
Robert Kaplan
The Ohio State University

**Physical Education Activities
Evaluation Materials Editor**

Jane A. Mott
Texas Woman's University

Cover photo by Max Winter

Copyright © 1972, 1977, 1981 by Wm. C. Brown Company
Publishers

Library of Congress Catalog Card Number: 80-67073

ISBN 0-697-07172-3

Printed in the United States of America
10   9   8   7

contents

preface

In writing this book the authors have two main objectives. The first is to provide the beginning racquetball player with an easy-to-follow sequence of playing techniques. The second objective is to instill an interest in a game that can not only be played by the student while in school but has a carry-over value into later life.

Before writing this new edition, the authors interviewed and discussed teaching techniques with many of the outstanding racquetball players in the country. These players included both the top male and female players. By doing this, it was hoped that a background of information could be complied that would provide a foundation for the basic instructional procedures utilized in teaching the game of racquetball.

It is amazing how much racquetball has progressed in the past few years. It wasn't too long ago that racquetball players had a difficult time finding a place to play, and little or no analysis of playing skills was available. The average players would find a court and then just bang away at the ball with little thought of either playing technique or game strategy. This textbook should fill the void for easy-to-understand instructions about racquetball.

The material in the text is organized in such a way that if a beginner follows the information in a step-by-step sequence, the player will soon not only know the basic skills but also the strategy that will dictate the use of each particular skill. Each skill is accompanied by sequence photographs that illustrate critical movements of the various strokes. Practice drills are given so that a person can develop individual techniques without outside supervision or instruction. Care has been taken to make all of the instructions as simple as possible. It is the hope of the authors that individuals who utilize this book will soon become a part of the large group of racquetball enthusiasts.

A section is included on the language of racquetball so that the student will be able to communicate intelligently with other racquetball players.

The self-evaluative questions placed throughout the chapters are designed to help the reader combine specific information into a meaningful whole. The questions are not always positioned according to the presentation of given topics. This is done so that each individual will have to stop and think about what has been learned at a certain point, and in addition, the questions become guidelines to future reading. As students develop skill in racquetball, they should return to any questions that originally gave them trouble until they can answer them with ease.

The material in this text has been and is being class tested with hundreds of students in beginning racquetball classes and is currently being utilized by many schools, racquetball clubs, and individuals interested in learning the basic skills of racquetball.

The authors feel that racquetball is one of the most enjoyable games now being played and hope that the reader will soon be in agreement.

what is
racquetball like?

1

The game of racquetball is one of American origin. It developed out of the game of paddleball in the late 1940s. Earl Riskey of the University of Michigan is credited with being the individual who came up with the original concepts of the game. While watching tennis players practice their shots in a handball court, he decided that one could play a game that was similar to handball, but would also include the skills of tennis. It was necessary to first use improvised equipment, such as tennis balls and paddle tennis racquets. The first rules of the game were adopted from handball and as the game spread, many local adaptations were added, especially in regard to the type of paddle racquet and ball utilized.

In 1949 Joe Sobek of Bridgeport, Connecticut, observed members of the Greenwich YMCA play a paddleball game in which a wooden paddle was used. He felt that the game could be improved by using a string racquet rather than a solid-faced wooden type, as the string racquet would afford better control and could impart better speed to the ball. The first ball was a pink rubber ball, similar to the inside of a tennis ball. In addition to this ball, Sobek developed a softer blue ball that was used by many players.

As players from the Greenwich YMCA moved to other parts of the country, they introduced the new game and the sport increased in popularity. Sobek was instrumental in the spread of the game, as he contributed equipment to various YMCAs so they could experiment with the new activity. As a result of these activities the sport spread rapidly during the years between 1949 and 1959.

In time the game was adopted by many YMCAs and recreation departments. Because of the inexpensive equipment and fast pace of the game many people become interested in playing racquetball. Since one can get an excellent workout in approximately thirty minutes, many businessmen were attracted to the game. They found that much of their daily tension and frustration could be expended and released on the racquetball court. Also all ages and both sexes find the game easy to learn. During this time, and into the 1960s, the game spread and was played under many different names, such as "paddle-rackets," "paddleball," and "paddle tennis." On April 26, 1969, players and officials attended an organizational meeting in St. Louis and selected a name that was felt to describe the game well. It was decided to officially adopt the name "racquetball" and the International Racquetball Association was formed. During this time the first International Racquetball Association Championships were held and now local, regional, and national championships are held for both men and women. The official organization for racquetball in this country is now known as the United States Racquetball Association and has its headquarters in Skokie, Illinois.

Since that time the popularity of the game has spread and one now finds players of all ages and both sexes playing racquetball. In order to become skilled in many activities, many hours of individual instruction and a great amount of practice time are required. The basic skills of racquetball, however, can be taught and learned in a relatively short period of time. The increase in interest, the development of facilities, and the addition of racquetball into physical education curricula have done much to promote the sport.

Racquetball is a fast game requiring endurance, skill, and body control. It requires the utilization of nearly all parts of the body. Because of its demands on the cardiorespiratory system, it ranks as an excellent conditioning activity. Research indicates that racquetball is an excellent means of providing the stimulus to bring about gains in endurance. Racquetball can help in the control of body weight because of the high caloric expenditure required in playing the game. In our sedentary type of society there is a need for physical activity to relieve the stress and tension of modern life. The fact that racquetball provides a means of relieving this tension makes it worthwhile in the development of good mental health. Racquetball, however, needs no outside justification, for it is a wonderful game to be enjoyed for itself.

Racquetball is an excellent activity because it doesn't require a great amount of time to get a vigorous workout. In just thirty minutes one can receive enough activity to gain many healthful benefits. In many areas it is played as an enjoyable corecreational activity, and the pace of the game is adjusted to meet the skill level and ages of the competitors. Racquetball is one of those rare sports where you can obtain a tremendous conditioning stimulus, but also have fun and total enjoyment at the same time.

Racquetball may be played by two (singles), three (cutthroat), or four (doubles) players. It may be played on a one-, three-, or four-walled court. Most of the information contained in this book applies to four-walled courts, but the basic strokes and shots also apply to one- and three-walled courts.

The game of racquetball does not require a lot of expensive equipment and can be played anywhere a court is available. The rules of the game are simple and easy to learn and one can become quite proficient in the basic skills in a short time. Many people continue to play racquetball until they are quite old, utilizing strategy and experience to offset their lack of speed and endurance.

PROCEDURE OF GAME

To start the game, the server stands within the service zone and, after letting the ball bounce once, strikes it, causing it to rebound off the front wall. In order to be in play, the ball must then land behind the short line. The server is given two attempts on the serve. If the first serve is not legal, then he is given another serve. The opponent must then return the ball in such a manner that it will hit the front wall before it strikes the floor, and play continues until either the serving or receiving side is unable to return the ball legally. A point is won by the serving side if the receiver returns the ball illegally. If the server fails to return the ball, he loses his serve. His opponent now becomes the server and the former server now becomes the receiver. A complete game ends when one side receives twenty-one points.

In doubles, each player is allowed to serve before a loss of team serve occurs, except in the case of the initial service, when only one player serves. Either player on the doubles team may return the ball after it is in play.

A match consists of the first two out of three games.

Figure 1.1 shows the measurements of four-, three-, and one-wall racquetball courts. The recommended four-wall court is 40 feet long and 20 feet wide, with a front wall of 20 feet and a back wall at least 12 feet high. The short line, parallel to the front wall, divides the playing court in half. The service line is parallel to and 5 feet in front of the short line. The area between these two lines is designated as the service zone. A service box is located at each end of the service zone. It is marked with lines 18 inches from each sidewall and the line is parallel to the sidewall. Five feet back of the short line, vertical lines are marked on each sidewall extending 3 inches from the floor. All lines are marked on the court with 1.5-inch-wide red or white lines.

The one-wall court has a front wall that is 20 feet in width and 16 feet high. The floor is 20 feet wide and the length is 34 feet from the front wall to the back edge of the long line. There should be a minimum of 6 feet beyond the long line and each sideline in order to provide movement area for the players. The short line is 16 feet from the front wall. Parallel with the short line and 9 feet back of it are markers designating the service line. The imaginary extension and joining of these lines on the floor indicates the service zone. The receiving zone is the floor area back of the short line bounded by and including the long and sidelines.

The three-wall dimensions are the same as the one-wall court, except that it has two sidewalls extending from the top of the front wall back along either sideline and slanting downward to a height of 6 feet at the short line, at which point they stop.

EQUIPMENT

Racquet

A short-handled racquet as shown in figure 1.2 must be utilized in racquetball. It is recommended that the racquet be approximately 8 inches wide and 17 inches in length. The length together with width may not exceed 27 inches

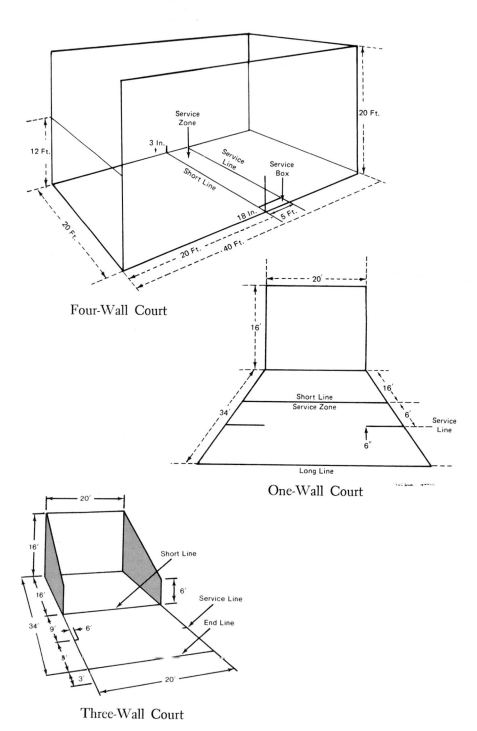

Fig. 1.1   Racquetball courts

Fig. 1.2   Racquets

and the weight should not exceed 16 ounces. Strings of the racquet may be gut, nylon, or metal.

It is required that a thong be attached to the handle and slipped over the wrist of the player during the game. During play the hands may become wet with perspiration; this thong will prevent the racquet from slipping from the hand and striking another player.

Ball

Many different balls are manufactured by individual companies. The United States Racquetball Association has recognized a ball developed by the Seamco Company and known as the black Seamco 558 as the official ball. The rules state that the ball should be 2.25 inches in diameter. It should weigh approximately 1.40 ounces and when dropped from a height of 100 inches, the bounce should be between 68 and 72 inches when the temperature is 76 F.

The type of ball used will determine to a great extent the speed of play. If one chooses to use a regular tennis ball, this will make for a fast-moving, hard-hitting style of play. It is suggested that the tennis ball be colored in order to make the ball easier to see.

Some balls are not as highly pressurized as a tennis ball and therefore do not travel as fast. The type of ball utilized in many cases will be determined by individual choice or local player acceptance.

Shoes and Socks

The comment that "the strength of an army lies in the feet of the soldier" is also true in racquetball. To avoid blisters and sore feet a player should make sure that he has good quality shoes that fit well. When purchasing a shoe, one should make sure that he is wearing the type of socks that he plans on wearing while playing racquetball and not regular street socks. This will insure a proper fit for the racquetball shoes. The sock should be white and made of soft material, such as wool or cotton, and must be kept clean to prevent infections, such as athlete's foot. If a player is bothered by sore feet, friction can be reduced by rubbing the soles of the feet with petroleum jelly or a good commercial skin lubricant.

Uniform

According to the official racquetball rules, all parts of the uniform, consisting of a shirt, shorts, and socks, shall be clean, and white or of bright colors. Warm-up pants or shirts, if worn in actual match play, shall also be white or of bright colors. Only club insignia, name of club, name of racquetball organization, name of tournament, or name of sponsor may be on the uniform. Players are not allowed to play without a shirt.

Accessory Equipment

In addition to the basic uniform of shoes, shorts, and shirts many players utilize other accessory equipment, such as a glove, wristbands, and headbands. The purpose of the racquet glove is to enable the player to obtain a firmer grip on the racquet during play. This is especially beneficial when moisture collects on the handle. By wearing wristbands and a headband the player can eliminate much of the moisture that might otherwise interfere with match play.

SAFETY

Safety is an important factor in the game of racquetball. One of the key areas of the body to protect is the face, especially the eyes. Generally, injuries to the eyes are the result of an unpredictable shot, a ricochet off the racquet, or just looking the wrong way and then being hit by the ball.

A number of protective devices for the eyes are available at a relatively inexpensive price. Figure 1.3 contains an example of some of the items that are currently on the market.

A few reminders will help you avoid being hit in the racquetball court.

1. Stay out of the path of the ball.
2. Protect your face.
3. Concentrate on what is taking place in the racquetball court.
4. Be aware of your opponent's position.

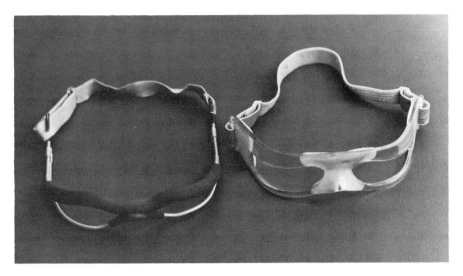

Fig. 1.3   Protective devices for eyes

WARM-UP

Many minor aches and pains can be eliminated by engaging in a pregame warm-up routine. Warming up is a process that allows the body temperature to increase, and thus achieve better muscular efficiency. Some of the physiological factors that are thought to be responsible for this increased efficiency are: (1) the muscle contracts and relaxes faster as a result of increased temperatures; (2) the oxygen-carrying molecules, hemoglobin in the blood and myoglobin in the muscle cell, release oxygen more readily as the body temperature increases; (3) the internal or viscous resistance inside the muscle is decreased, also the resistance to blood flow in the circulatory vessels is thought to be reduced; and (4) the metabolic activity of the cell mechanisms increase, which is thought to be a factor that could contribute to a better release of energy.

Electrocardiographic tracings of people engaging in strenuous activity without the use of a warm-up showed abnormal waves during the first minutes of exercise. These abnormal waves were absent when the exercise bout was preceded by a warm-up period of just two minutes.

A good way to start your warm-up period is through the use of stretching exercises. This will increase your flexibility and reduce the chance of muscle and joint injury. Racquetball is a game of mobility, quickness, and rapid change of direction. A few minutes of basic stretching exercises can

Can you name at least six safety procedures that should always be observed while playing racquetball?

contribute to being loose and ready to play. Most people tend to lack flexibility in the posterior thigh, anterior hip, low back, and chest—muscle groups that contribute much to the playing of racquetball.

The type of movement used in a stretching program is very important. Receptors located in the muscles and joints are stimulated by specific kinds of stretching movements. If you use fast, jerky, bouncy movements, this causes the muscle you are attempting to stretch to contract at the same time. This reduces the effectiveness of your stretching and often causes muscle soreness.

By using a slow, sustained stretch, the receptors cause the muscle to relax and lengthen, and thus aid in obtaining increased flexibility. Much of the muscle soreness is prevented or alleviated by this type of movement. When performing the recommended stretching exercises, you should remember to use a slow, sustained stretch.

In some cases you may find that some uncomfortable stiffness and soreness may develop in approximately twenty-four hours after you first start to play racquetball. This is due to the fact that you are probably starting to use muscles that haven't been involved in your other daily activities. By engaging in a stretching program, you can get rid of much of this discomfort.

Figures 1.4—1.11 contain descriptions of some basic stretching exercises that can be used by racquetball players.

After you have completed your stretching, use the game of racquetball for the rest of your warm-up. You will not only warm up, but you will also be increasing your shot ability at the same time.

While you are warming up, think about the correct position of your body that is necessary to hit the ball in a proper manner. Get the feel of the racquet and the feel of all of your shots. You can avoid many mistakes by using the pregame time as a mental warm-up as well as a physiological warm-up.

Fig. 1.4   Sitting toe-touch

Muscles stretched: Hamstrings.
Starting position: Sit on the floor with the legs straight and together.
Action: Extend the arms forward toward the toes, palms up. Stretch to or beyond the toes until stretch pain is felt. Hold 3-5 seconds. Return to starting position.
Precautions: Do not bob. Keep the knees straight.

Fig. 1.5   Indian curl

Muscles stretched: Back extensors.
Starting position: Sit with the legs crossed and arms folded or relaxed.
Action: Tuck the chin and curl forward attempting to touch the forehead to the knees. Hold 3-5 seconds. Return to starting position.
Precautions: Do not bob. Keep the hips on the floor.

Fig. 1.6   Knee-chest curl

Muscles stretched: Low back extensors.
Starting position: Lie on back.
Action: Bring both knees to the chest, grabbing just under the knees and pulling the knees toward the armpits. Hold 5 seconds. Return to starting position.
Precautions: Avoid pulling with the knees together.

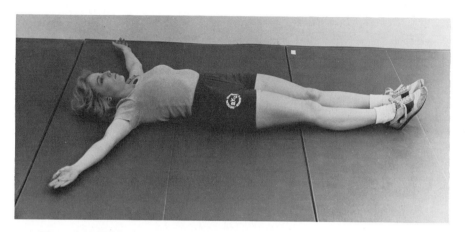

Fig. 1.7 Leg-over

Muscles stretched: Trunk rotators.
Starting position: Lie on the back with the arms extended to the side at shoulder level.
Action: Raise the left leg to a vertical position, keeping the leg straight.

Twist the body to touch the left leg to the right hand. Hold 3-5 seconds. Return to starting position. Repeat to opposite side.
Precautions: Keep the knees straight. Keep the arms and trunk on the floor.

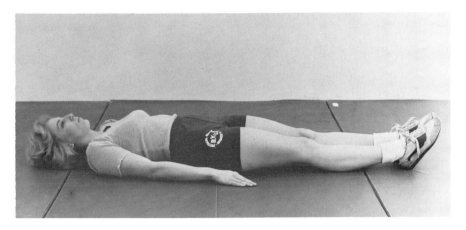

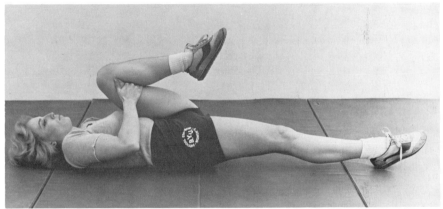

Fig. 1.8 Lying knee-pull

Muscles stretched: Hip flexors.
Starting position: Lie on the back with the legs extended.
Action: Bring the left knee to the chest, grabbing just under the knee with both hands. Pull until a stretch pain is felt. Hold 3-5 seconds. Return to starting position. Repeat to opposite side.
Precaution: Keep the extended leg straight and on the floor. Stretch slowly.

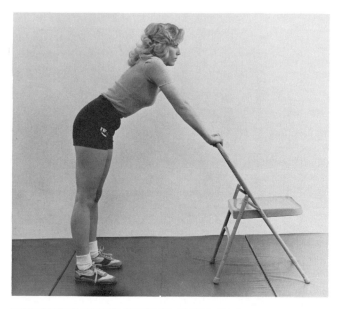

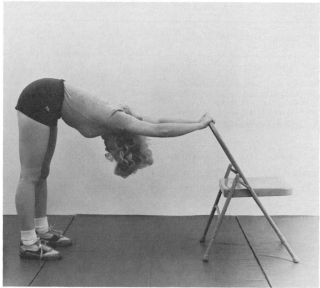

Fig. 1.9   Chair stretch

Muscles stretched: Pectoral muscles.
Starting position: Stand with feet apart (sideways) facing the back of the chair. Reach forward and place both hands on the chair back.
Action: Draw the head and chest downward by contracting the abdominal muscles. Hold 3-5 seconds. Return to starting position.
Precautions: Keep the feet spread and well back from the chair. Keep the lower back flat with no arch.

Fig. 1.10   Heel-cord stretch

Muscles stretched: Heel cord, gastro-cnemius, soleus.

Starting position: Stand facing the wall with the palms against the wall and the body at arm's length. Spread the feet apart slightly.

Action: Keeping the feet flat and the body in a straight line, lean forward allowing the elbows to bend slightly until a stretch pain is felt in the calf muscles. Hold 3-5 seconds. Return to starting position.

Precautions: Keep the knees and body straight and the feet flat. For more stretch, put a book under the balls of the feet.

Fig. 1.11   Billig stretch

Muscles stretched: Muscles and ligaments of the pelvic girdle.
Starting position: Stand with feet together and right side to wall, about 18 inches from the wall. Place right hand and forearm against the wall at shoulder level. Place the heel of the left hand on the buttocks.
Action: Keeping the body straight and facing forward, move the hips forward and inward to the wall below the hand by contracting the abdominal and gluteal (buttock) muscles and pushing with the left hand. Return to starting position. Repeat to opposite side.
Precautions: Keep the knees straight. Keep the hips and shoulders facing forward.

How can you tell whether you have warmed up or cooled down sufficiently?

The best indicator that the body is in a warmed condition is the onset of perspiration. The time you spend in warming up will be well worth the time and effort.

COOL DOWN

A person should also be aware of the need for cooling down after a strenuous racquetball workout. Muscles sometimes tighten up and even go into painful spasms. This can be prevented or reduced by tapering off and allowing the body to return to a normal level of metabolic activity before going to the shower.

A series of one-way valves are located in the veins of the circulatory system in order to permit the flow of blood in only one direction. In order to assist the blood in circulating, you should taper off gradually by walking or jogging slowly for a few minutes. As the muscles contract during the cool-down period, they create pressure against the veins, which in turn aids in the return of blood to the heart. Without this cool-down period, the blood might pool in the lower body.

A general indicator is to cool down until you have stopped sweating profusely and the heart rate has dropped to 100 beats per minute or less.

essential skills
2

It is very important in learning to play racquetball to use good form. Good form will enable a player to play a better game by hitting the ball harder; the ball can also be directed as desired. One will get much more fun and personal satisfaction from the game of racquetball if good form is utilized.

Control of the ball is lost if strokes are awkward, cramped, and jerky and if the racquet is constantly pushed in front of the body instead of making a free swing at one's side. The placing of the wrong foot forward will throw the body off balance. A really good player will correct these faults.

A player can avoid these common mistakes in swing and footwork if he will carefully follow the advice and recommendations given in this book. All of the instructions will be given for right-handed players.

WRIST ACTION

One of the important causes of error in racquetball is the improper position of the wrist when hitting the racquetball strokes. If you keep the wrist too stiff, the result is that the ball is pushed rather than stroked toward the front wall. This type of movement will decrease the amount of power you will be able to put on the ball.

One way to obtain the proper wrist position is to think of the action of a cobra as it is getting ready to strike. The wrist is held in a cocked back position at the start of the stroke and at the moment of contact is snapped or uncocked in order to impart maximum power on the ball. This is a coordinated movement that begins at the shoulder, moves to the wrist, and finally moves to the ball at impact. Figure 2.1 contains an example of this important concept.

STANCE (Fig. 2.2)

In racquetball the ready position is assumed prior to hitting any stroke. This position should be maintained while one faces the front wall until the ball is approaching the player. Now as the ball approaches you can pivot toward

Fig. 2.1   "Cobra" wrist action

Fig. 2.2   Ready position

the approaching ball and prepare to hit either a forehand or backhand shot. It is important that the weight be distributed on the balls of the feet while the ball is in play. At no time should the player stand flat-footed. At all times the knees should be slightly bent so that playing position is a low position with the back kept straight. Many times players feel that they are getting low by bending the back rather than the knees.

THE FOREHAND STROKE (Fig. 2.3)

The forehand stroke is a fundamental stroke in racquetball. This is the stroke that enables one to keep the ball in play. It allows a player to get into the proper position after the ball has been hit and eventually enables the player to position himself to put the ball away, or to get the ball past the opponent. The forehand stroke is a very natural stroke and in its simplest form it is accomplished by drawing the racquet back until it points towards the back wall, then drawing it forward to meet the ball knee-high.

Grip

To be able to swing the racquet back and then forward to meet the ball, a player first of all needs to know how to hold the racquet properly. The grip that is recommended is known as the "handshake" grip.

Stand the edge of the frame of the racquet on a table or on the floor with the handle pointing towards the body. Now, shake hands with the handle so that the **V** formed by the thumb and index finger is directly on top of the racquet handle. The thumb and fingers will overlap the handle so that both the thumb and fingers will close around the handle in a comfortable manner. You should have the index finger extended slightly, and the heel of the palm should touch the very end of the racquet, parallel with the end of the racquet but not overlapping. The palm of the hand will now be in the same plane as the face of the racquet.

Fig. 2.3   The forehand stroke

Fig. 2.3—Continued

Backswing

In order to execute a good forehand drive in tennis, a long swing is necessary to generate more speed. In racquetball, however, the swing must be shortened in order to move the racquet fast enough to make contact with the ball, due to the smaller court area. You can still generate good speed and power by shortening the swing if you remember to use the proper wrist action. As the ball approaches, the racquet is drawn back with the wrist fully cocked, and the racquet around head height or slightly higher. The left arm is slightly in front of the body and the knees are slightly bent with the back in a fairly straight position. The body is turned so that your nonhitting shoulder is now facing the front wall.

Forward Swing

As the racquet is swung forward, the body weight is shifted from the right foot to the left foot. This is accomplished by stepping out with the left leg about 13 to 20 inches as you transfer the weight to the front foot. As you stride into the ball, you should dip the hitting shoulder to help lower the racquet. As you swing into the ball, the right knee bends and the left arm starts to pull the body through the stroke. As the forward swing continues, the wrist remains in a cocked position with the racquet pointing backwards. The right arm is bent at the elbow and tucked in close to the side of the body. The body is now in a position to generate tremendous power at the time of impact.

Impact

The most important movement in the forward swing is when the racquet meets the ball. Contact is made with the ball off from the front foot. Just before you make impact, you should snap the wrist forward so that the racquet face is vertical and traveling in a straight line into the ball. If you have enough time, you should let the ball drop as low as you can before hitting it. This will allow you to keep it low on the front wall. You can accomplish a low hitting position by bending the knees, dropping the hitting shoulder, and pivoting the hips into the shot. It is also important to emphasize the need to maintain visual contact with the ball during the stroke in order to assure a proper stroke. This helps you to keep the head down through impact and insures a powerful but accurate shot.

Follow-Through

As the wrist is snapped through the ball, the left arm moves out of the way to pull the body through the final part of the stroke. The body remains low, with bent legs, until the stroke is completed. The racquet continues up behind the left side of the head. It is important that you maintain good balance at the end of the stroke so that you can quickly move in any direction in order to be ready to play your opponent's return shot.

THE BACKHAND STROKE (Fig. 2.4)

In order to become a proficient racquetball player, you must have a good backhand stroke. At first this stroke may feel uncomfortable, but by utilizing the proper techniques and body position, you can with practice learn a backhand stroke that will be both accurate and powerful.

Grip

If you have enough time, it is best to switch the grip from the forehand grip to a backhand grip. This is accomplished by moving the hand to the left on the handle until the **V** formed by the thumb and index finger is directly on top of the left diagonal of the racquet handle. See figure 2.4 for an indication of the proper position for the backhand. By practicing this change, you will find that it will be possible to switch grips quite rapidly. It is important to point out that you should not use the nonhitting hand to assist you in changing grips, as this will interfere with your swing and slow you down.

Sometimes in the course of playing, especially when you hit shots in the front court or on the fly before the ball bounces, you will not have time to switch from a forehand grip. In this case, you want to make sure that the racquet face is in a vertical plane at the time of impact with the ball. This type of grip will cut down on the power of your backhand, so try to hit as accurate a shot as possible.

Stance

The stance for the backhand drive is the exact opposite of that for the forehand drive. As the ball approaches a player's backhand, the body pivots to the left facing the left sidewall. This is accomplished by stepping forward toward the ball, with the right foot pointing diagonally toward the left sidewall. Body

Fig. 2.4   The backhand stroke

Fig. 2.4—Continued

position should be such that the right shoulder points toward the front wall and the left shoulder points toward the back wall. The right foot will be toward the front wall and ahead of the left foot. The feet should run in a parallel line to the left sideline. As one steps forward with the right foot, weight should also be forward on this foot with the knees slightly bent, putting the weight on the balls of the feet.

Backswing

In setting up for the shot, it is important to get the racquet back as quickly as possible. This will keep you from using a short, punching type of stroke. As the racquet is pulled back, the wrist is fully cocked. One way to check to see if the wrist is cocked is to make sure the racquet head is up and in line with the forearm. This puts the racquet in the proper position for a powerful stroke. The hitting arm is bent at the elbow and the knees are in a bent position, with the shoulders rotated, so that the racquet is approximately head high. The body is now in position for the forward swing.

Forward Swing and Impact

At the completion of the backswing, it is necessary to start swinging the racquet forward toward the ball. You do this by stepping forward and shifting the weight to the front leg. As you do this, the hitting arm starts to extend, but the racquet is still back with the wrist in a cocked position. This is accomplished by rotating the shoulders and pivoting the hips into the shot. Just before you make contact with the ball, the hitting arm is nearly extended and the wrist is starting to snap as the shoulder pulls the racquet through the stroke. Contact with the ball is made off from the front foot, and at the moment of impact the hitting arm is fully extended and the wrist snaps through the ball. The elbow of the hitting arm is about 6 to 10 inches from the body at the moment of impact. It is important to keep your eyes on the ball at all times in order to maintain a proper body position. Even though the wrist snaps through the ball, it should be vertical at impact and shouldn't roll over as you hit the ball. This will help to maintain accuracy along with the power.

Follow-Through

As contact with the ball is made, the racquet should follow through to the right side of the body. In the beginning of the follow-through, the wrist is held firm and the racquet is still horizontal to give maximum direction to the shot. The legs remain bent in order to keep the body low. The hitting shoulder is pulled through and the racquet continues on a horizontal plane at about waist height for a complete follow-through. Always maintain good body balance so that you are ready to move to a position for a return shot.

THE CONTINENTAL GRIP

The authors believe that all beginners should start using the "handshake," grip that has been described previously in this chapter. This grip allows the beginner to completely close all of the fingers with the thumb locked on the first finger, which we feel will give the player a tighter grip as well as good control of the racquet. However, as players advance in their skill, technique, and experience in racquetball, they may want to vary that grip somewhat. Another grip with slight variation from the handshake grip is the Continental grip. The one advantage of this grip over the handshake grip is that it allows a player to hit the forehand and backhand with basically the same grip and with very little change or adjustment. Therefore, it will reduce the problems of changing grips whenever the player is forced to hit the ball quickly and in changing from one stroke to another during a rally.

Forehand (Fig. 2.5)

To assume the forehand grip, the player would use the same procedure as explained previously in assuming the handshake grip, with the only difference being that the index finger, or the first finger, is now squarely against the back of the handle rather than curling around into a locked position with the thumb, as explained in the handshake grip. What this allows is more of a finger spread on the grip, as opposed to the total closed finger position that is required for the handshake grip. Therefore, this would possibly give better control, inasmuch as you have more range of motion covered on the racquet handle.

You will note in looking down at your grip now that a **V** has been formed by the thumb and first finger on top of the racquet handle or slightly to the left edge of the grip. Please note that the thumb is now curled over the handle to lock against the second finger, as the first finger, or index finger, is now against the back of the handle and grip.

The other mechanics of the Continental forehand stroke, such as stance, backswing, forward swing, impact, and follow-through, would be exactly the same as explained and illustrated in the handshake forehand.

Backhand

The same grip used for the forehand can also be used for the backhand with very little adjustment. The proper placement of the grip is illustrated in figure 2.6. In looking down at your racquet and grip you should see a **V** formed on the top part of the handle when the racquet is held perpendicular to the floor. The **V** should be to the left of the center of the grip. The fingers must be held tightly together to maintain both good control and power. This grip may be assumed by slightly shifting or turning the hand to the left so that all the fingers now come together and so that the thumb is spread diagonally on the backside of the racquet handle. This grip differs from the handshake

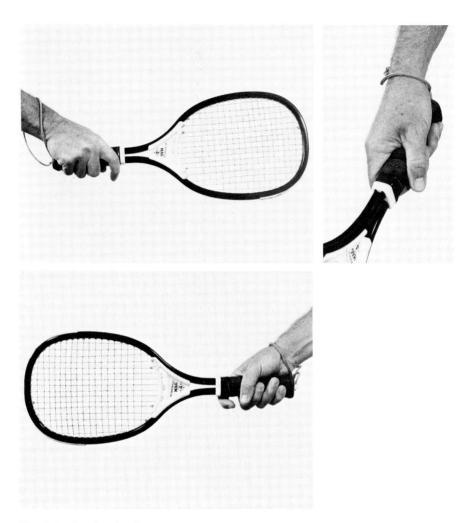

Fig. 2.5 Forehand grip

backhand grip in that the knuckles on the hand do not point upwards toward the ceiling as much and the thumb stretches diagonally along the backside of the grip rather than parallel to it. The value of this grip over the handshake grip is that the adjustment can be made more quickly.

Again, the mechanics of the Continental backhand stroke, such as stance, backswing, forward swing, impact, and follow-through, are the same as the handshake backhand.

Regardless of what grip you use, the important thing to remember relative to the grip is to have total control of the racquet and to feel comfortable with it.

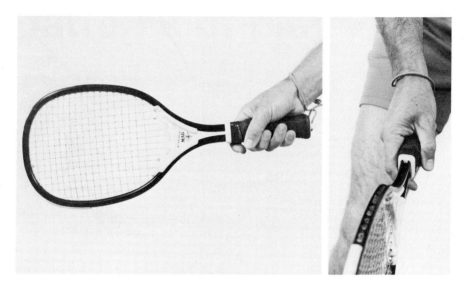

Fig. 2.6 Backhand grip

THE IMPORTANCE OF KEEPING ONE'S EYES ON THE BALL

In most sports keeping one's eyes on the ball at all times when the ball is in play is a vital and important factor. Such is the case in racquetball. A player must keep his eyes on the ball or watch the ball into the center of the racquet in order to hit the ball at exactly the right moment to generate speed and, most important, placement and direction. It is vital to look at the ball even to the point of looking at the spot where the ball was after the racquet has made contact and has hit the ball on its flight forward. The follow-through of the swing pulls the body and eyes around so that the body is now facing the front wall and can pick up the direction of the ball from this follow-through motion. If a player cheats by taking the eyes off the ball a split second before making contact with it, the player will not be able to execute a good shot with adequate speed or proper direction.

The racquet should be examined after it has been used a number of times to see that the strings are getting the most use in the center of the racquet. If this is the case, then the ball is surely being hit in the proper place. The important key to playing a successful racquetball game is in watching the ball, not the opponent or any part of one's own body or swing. A constant eye should be kept on the ball throughout the playing of a match. This will allow for a determination of the ball's speed, and bounce and the way it must be played on a return.

It is a common fault of most beginners to turn both their head and body toward the back wall after they have stroked the ball to see where the ball has landed and to watch their opponent return the ball to the front wall. In doing this, the player puts himself out of position to be ready for the next shot, as well as taking the chance of being hit in the face by the returned ball. He also

---

Can you take the correct forehand grip, hit the ball to the front wall, and then change to the backhand grip to make a successful return? Using forehand strokes, can you stroke the ball continually to the front wall 6 times without missing? 12 times? 20 times? Can you do the same number of hits alternating forehand and backhand strokes?

---

faces the chance of getting beat by the returning ball by being out of position and having to make a complete turn to the front wall.

In order for the shot to be good, the ball must return to the front wall; therefore, this turn toward the back wall is totally wasted and could cost the player either a point or a side out.

THE SERVE

The serve is very important in the game of racquetball, as every point begins with the serve. This is the only stroke in the game that enables a player to take enough time to observe the position of the opponent and to get ready for the return stroke. Thus, this time is a definite advantage.

The serve should be used by beginners with the same philosophy used in learning the forehand and backhand strokes. Accuracy is developed before speed. One of the most common mistakes of the beginning player is to try to hit the ball too hard. One must realize that competent players who hit the ball with ease and speed have probably played the game for many years and consequently they make it look easy because of the experience they have had on the court. However, all of these players started by placing the ball accurately before applying complete speed to their drives, smashes, and serves. Speed must be increased gradually only after the point where the ball is consistently hit to the frontcourt and placed on the frontcourt as desired. If a beginner tries to hit the ball too hard he will simply delay his improvement, and skill will come much slower.

The serve in its simplest form merely puts the ball in play, but a strong, well-placed serve gives a player a fine opportunity to get an advantage on his opponent; he can and should make full use of this advantage.

There are four different basic types of serves in racquetball—the drive serve, the garbage serve, the lob serve, and the Z-serve. The most used serve is the drive serve. This is the serve that will be most used when a beginner develops playing skills and becomes proficient in the game. However, even with the best players and the best servers, there comes a time in everyone's game when the drive serve may not be landing as it should. It may be off just a degree so that the opponent is returning it to the front wall with ease. It is at this time that you might feel the need to change to a different serve in order to make the game competitive. Two serves that can be very effective are the lob serve and the garbage serve. These serves can be used without excessive power or strength and can give a player a period of recovery or rest during the match if the player tires at any time. The Z-serve is a more difficult serve to master, but it has the advantage of hitting a multiple of walls, and if your opponent is confused by the way the ball rebounds off the wall, it can be very effective.

One important point to remember when serving is to stand in approximately the center of the serving area. If you stand too close to either sidewall, you will be giving up the most important center court position. Also you won't be able to serve the ball to either side of the court.

Assuming that you have executed the serve correctly, where might the ball travel that would result in a fault?

Serve the majority of the time to your opponent's weakness, which in most instances is the backhand. This will limit the ability to hit a strong return and will allow you to control the game.

In serving, you must first bounce the ball before hitting it, and the ball must then strike the front wall before making contact with the sidewalls. The ball must pass the short line on the fly to be good and if you hit three walls, including the front wall, on the fly, the serve is a fault. Any serve that hits either the ceiling or the back wall after hitting the front wall is also a fault. Two consecutive faults result in a loss of serve, and any serve that hits a wall before contacting the front wall is an out.

THE DRIVE SERVE (Fig. 2.7)

The serve that determines a consistent winner is the drive serve. Slow serves either result in long rallies or give your opponent an opportunity to take the offensive. The drive serve produces aces, or your opponent may hit a weak return and thus give you an excellent chance to win the point.

The service stroke should be delivered with a free, rhythmic swing in a continuous motion. A complete range of motion can be utilized on the serve, whereas in the forehand and backhand strokes the speed of the ball will sometimes dictate the use of a short rather than a full swing. The service should be smooth, uncramped, and without a hitch. In order to get power in a serve, your body weight must be put behind the ball by shifting the body weight forward. By using a proper backswing and forward swing, the racquet has time to pick up speed and should be traveling at its fastest speed when it contacts the ball

Stance

To begin the serve, the body is turned to the right so that it is facing the right wall. The left shoulder should be in line with the front wall and the right shoulder in line with the back wall. The right foot is in front of the left foot and the right leg is slightly bent and the left leg bent a little more than the right leg. The arms are fully extended and the ball is held against the racquet. During this time of the serve, look at the ball and visualize mentally how you plan to hit the ball on the serve.

Fig. 2.7   The drive serve

Grip

The grip for the serve is the same grip used for the forehand stroke. The most used grip is the "handshake" grip, as described previously. As contact is made with the ball on the serve, the hand should grip the racquet handle tightly. It is said that a good player squeezes a little "sawdust" out of the end of the racquet as contact is made with the ball.

Dropping the Ball

Once the service stance has been assumed facing the right sidewall with knees slightly bent, the left arm and hand are extended, holding the ball immediately in front of the body and toward the right sideline, in a straight line opposite the chest or slightly below. Now the ball can be dropped to the floor from this position just as though it was a rock or an egg dropping from the hand. The ball will have sufficient bounce in order to hit it, so it is not necessary to throw the ball; rather, it drops from the hand position. As the ball hits the floor and bounces upward, the backswing must be coordinated with the shifting of weight from the left foot to the back foot.

Backswing

As has been previously mentioned, a full swing is necessary in order to generate speed and power. The further back the racquet is drawn, the longer the forward swing will be and the faster the racquet will be moving when it hits the ball. As the ball comes up from the floor, the racquet is drawn back as far as can be comfortably done with the elbow bent. As the racquet is drawn back, weight is shifted from the left foot to the right foot. This is the position in which to make a forward swing. Notice how the racquet is cocked in order to generate power with the wrist at impact.

Forward Swing and Impact

As the racquet is swung forward, the weight is shifted from the right foot to the left foot as you stride into the ball. At the moment of impact the left leg extends forward and the right knee is bent, in order for the hitting shoulder to drop as you pivot into the ball with your right hip.

The timing of the drive serve should be such that the ball is hit below knee level. As the ball nears the floor, the hitting wrist drops low and the arm straightens out with a full wrist snap through the ball.

You should aim for a spot on the front wall about three feet up and one foot to the left of the center of the front wall to serve to the backhand and three feet up and one foot to the right of the center of the front wall to serve to the forehand.

Follow-Through

The follow-through is important. After the racquet has hit the ball, it should follow through forward and then to the left of the body. No attempt should be made to check the forward swing of the racquet or the forward motion of the body after the ball has left the racquet. The follow-through of the swing should pull the body forward and around so that it is now in good playing position to receive the ball as it is hit back to the front wall by the opponent.

DRIVE SERVE VARIATIONS

Backhand and Forehand (Fig. 2.8)

These two variations of the drive serve are the most common and effective of all the serves in racquetball. The ball is hit hard to the front wall and slightly off the center. It should travel fast toward the rear corner and be low enough to rebound off the floor. The ball should be hit low enough to prevent any rebound from the back wall. This forces an opponent to return the ball after the rebound. Even if the ball is hit high, but close to the sidewall, the rebound will be such that an opponent will be forced to swing from a crowded or bent-arm position. At all times one should attempt to achieve good serve placement and direction, in order to inhibit an opponent's swing.

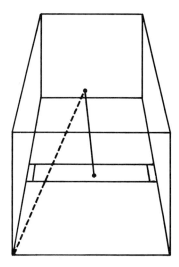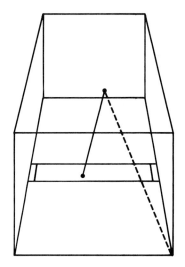

Fig. 2.8   Drive serves

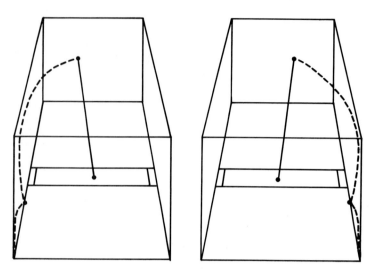

Fig. 2.9 Garbage serves

THE GARBAGE SERVE (Fig. 2.9)

Earlier in the chapter, the necessity and advantage of having more than one serve was mentioned. The drive serve is the most used serve, but it is felt that a player needs other serves combined with the drive serve. Such a serve is the garbage serve. It can be very effective in different situations and at certain times during a match. The garbage serve is hit in the air above your opponent's head. The serve should be placed as high and as close to the wall and back corner as possible, so that the opponent has difficulty making a full swing at the ball when returning it to the front wall.

The stroke is a push rather than the hard and powerful stroke used in the drive serve.

Stance

Assume the same type of stance as in the drive serve. In order to disguise your serve, you want to start all of your serves in the same manner, otherwise your opponent will be able to anticipate the serve and be able to adjust quickly in order to hit a better return.

Dropping the Ball

In dropping the ball, you need to allow the ball to rebound so that the rebound peaks at about chest height.

Backswing

As you bring the racquet back, use a backswing similar to the drive serve, except the body is more erect and the knees are not bent as much, as you will be hitting the ball at a higher arc in the garbage serve.

Forward Swing and Impact

As the racquet is swung forward, the weight is shifted from the right foot to the left foot, the knees are slightly bent, and the body leans forward toward the ball. Notice that the body is still more erect than in the drive serve. This allows you to make contact with the ball at a higher arc. You must not get too close to the ball. When contact is made at a point between the waist and the chest, the stroke is a push toward the front wall. Allow the racquet face to tilt backward as you make contact with the ball, and this will cause the ball to travel in an upward direction. Aim for a spot midway up the front wall and approximately one foot to either the left or right of the center of the front wall. The ball should now rebound about 5 feet behind the short line and then bounce upward and drop into the back corner.

Follow-Through

As the racquet makes contact with the ball, the body should be moving forward toward the ball and the weight should be shifting to the left foot. After the racquet has hit the ball it should follow through forward and upward so that the racket is now immediately overhead in a straight line and slightly to the left. If the player wishes the serve to be shorter and not as high in nature, then it is necessary to check the forward swing before it gets to its final position. Follow-through is not as important as it is in the drive serve, as the body is already facing the front wall and the player is in good position to recover and receive the ball as it is hit back to the front wall by his opponent.

GARBAGE SERVE VARIATIONS

Backhand and Forehand

The ball is hit high on the front wall slightly off the center and in such a manner that it makes a high bounce to the rear corner of the court. The force on the ball should cause the ball to just reach the back wall after rebounding from the floor. From this rebound the ball should then drop down, making it extremely difficult to swing at.

By effectively placing the ball with a high bounce close to the sidewall, your opponent will have a difficult time in making a full swing.

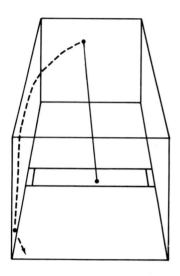

Fig. 2.10   Lob serve

LOB SERVE (Fig. 2.10)

The lob serve is a higher version of the garbage serve and utilizes the sidewall on the downward trajectory.

The serve is hit exactly like the garbage serve, except that you aim at a spot about three-fourths of the way up on the front wall and a foot to the left or right of the center of the front wall. This will determine whether the lob will go to either the forehand or the backhand. As the ball rebounds from the front wall, it should strike the sidewall about 6 feet up from the floor and about 6 feet in front of the back wall. By making contact with the sidewall, you will be able to keep the ball from rebounding hard off the back wall and giving your opponent an easy shot.

Since it is important that the ball hit the side wall as it descends, the lob serve is usually a more difficult serve to control than the garbage serve. Also, since you serve the ball with a higher elevation, the ball is in the air longer and your opponent may anticipate the serve and hit it on the fly for a strong offensive return.

Although the lob serve can be very effective, there are two disadvantages. Can you name them?

Z-SERVE

The Z-serve gets its name from the pattern the ball traverses during the flight from the front wall to the rear corner of the court. It is an especially effective serve against players who have a hard time following the flight of the ball and do not read the rebound of the ball off the wall very well. The Z-serve can be hit to either the backhand or the forehand. The Z-serve can be used either as a low Z-serve or a high Z-serve. In Z-serves, you take a serving position a few feet to the center of the service zone.

Low Z-Serve (Fig. 2.11)

The low Z-serve is hit the same way as the drive serve. The most effective low Z-serve is one that is hit to the backhand. Aim for a spot on the front wall about 3 to 4 feet up on the front wall and about 1 foot in from the right sidewall. After hitting the front wall, the ball should travel into the right sidewall and then travel across the playing court into the left rear corner, where it strikes the floor and then rebounds about 4 feet up from the floor and 4 feet from the back wall.

If the ball is served properly, the amount of spin placed on the ball will cause it to come off the left sidewall parallel to the back wall. This is a very difficult shot to return and leaves the person returning the shot in poor court position.

High Z-Serve (Fig. 2.12)

The high Z-serve is a change-of-pace serve, and the stroke for this serve is more like the push stroke used in the garbage serve. The ball is served with about 50 percent power to a spot about 12 to 15 feet up on the front wall and 1 foot from the sidewall. It will then rebound into the sidewall and travel with a high arching motion toward the rear corner and strike the floor, then hit the sidewall with little speed, and drop in the corner near the back wall.

The benefit of the high Z-serve is that if your opponent does not hit the serve before it bounces on the floor, it will die against the back wall. This serve can be hit to your opponent's forehand quite effectively.

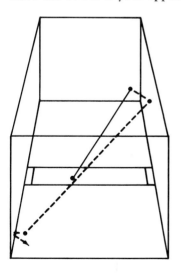

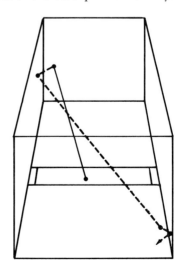

Fig. 2.11   Low Z-serve   Fig. 2.12   High Z-serve

OVERHEAD SMASH (Fig. 2.13)

The overhead smash in racquetball is made with practically the same swing as that used in the serve in tennis. However, as there is no net to contend with in racquetball and since the ball can land practically three feet closer to the floor, it is not necessary to put a slice or cut on the ball.

In racquetball the ball is hit with a flat racquet face, as opposed to cutting or slicing the ball. The smash is utilized when the ball comes off the front wall to the player in such a manner that it is high and above the head.

Beginners should not worry about developing the overhead smash until all other phases of the game have been developed. Every ball, regardless of how high it might be in coming, will always drop down to a position where the forehand or backhand drive can be used.

It is not necessary to have a smash in order to be a good racquetball player, but if a person has had some experience with it, there are certain times and instances where it can improve the overall game.

This stroke should be executed with the same type of motion as the forehand, backhand, and drive serve strokes. It should be a continuous motion, a rhythmic swing without pause. Since the stroke utilizes a backswing, an upward swing, a forward swing, and a follow-through, one must remember that, in order for it to be effective, the stroke must be used with a long, free swing.

Fig. 2.13 Overhead smash

Fig. 2.13—Continued

Grip

The grip for the overhead smash is primarily the same as the handshake fore-hand grip. A good player can utilize this grip and be very effective with the overhead smash. However, if the oncoming ball does allow enough time to make a slight shift in grip, it is desirable to use a grip that falls somewhere between the handshake forehand grip and the backhand grip. This is accomplished by:

1. Shaking hands with the handle of the racquet as is done in the forehand grip.
2. Shifting the palm one-eighth of a turn to the left instead of the one-fourth turn for the backhand grip.
3. The hand should be at the end of the racquet handle and wrapped around the handle so that the thumb touches the first finger.

Stance

The stance for the overhead smash is a diagonal stance toward the front wall. The left foot should point diagonally toward the front wall and the right foot is somewhat pointed toward the right wall. Weight should be evenly distributed on both feet and as the backward swing is started, weight should shift to the right foot. Then, as the upward swing is begun, the weight should be shifted to the left foot. In taking the proper position for the smash, the left shoulder should be pointing toward the front wall and the right shoulder toward the back wall.

Backswing

As the right arm is drawn down, the racquet is pulled away from the left hand, which has been acting as a balancer for control. The racquet should be pulled straight down, close to the body and to the right foot. As the racquet is drawn down, body weight is shifted from the left foot back to the right foot. The backward swing continues until the arm is fully extended and as far back as it can comfortably be drawn.

Upward Swing

Now the racquet is ready to be drawn upward and as this is done, the elbow is bent in order to impart speed and power to the swing. Also, bending the elbow will help to hit the ball high in the air and directly over the right eye, the ideal place to make contact with the ball. If the elbow is not bent, the shot will lack the power a player is trying to achieve. Bending the elbow also increases the accuracy of the shot.

After bending the elbow, the racquet is carried upward until the handle is to the right of the ear. This will put the racquet in position to begin the forward swing.

Forward Swing

As the racquet starts forward, the elbow is gradually straightened out, as it is desirable to hit the ball directly over the right eye with the arm fully extended and the ball as high in the air as can be reached with this full extension. As the racquet swings forward, weight is shifted from the right foot forward to the left foot. This will enable the body to move forward with the complete swing. One should remember at all times to coordinate the backward, upward, and forward swing in one smooth motion without any pause.

Impact

The ball can be hit effectively with a flat racquet face, without cutting across the ball. By hitting it with the flat racquet face, much speed and power can be generated. The main thing to remember in meeting the ball is that contact be made when the ball is high above the right eye with the arm fully extended. Coordination of the entire swing, so that the ball is met at the proper time, is the key to making the smash successful.

One common fault of novice players is to pull back as they make contact with the ball. Can you explain why this reduces power and may affect the direction of the hit?

Follow-Through

After contact has been made with the ball, the racquet is allowed to follow through forward toward the front wall and down across the body to the left side. The momentum of the racquet follow-through should completely pull the right foot up and forward, so that the body is now facing the front wall and in position for the opponent's return of the ball.

Once a player has mastered the essential skills he is ready to utilize them in perfecting all of the shots in racquetball.

HELPFUL HINTS FOR THE BEGINNER

Even a beginning racquetball player can usually stand back and make a logical assessment of his mistakes—what went wrong during that part of his game where he has made a mistake. It is a fairly easy game in which to analyze what you are doing wrong and to determine how to correct the things that need correcting. When play is not going as it should, there are some essential skills the player can check for proper execution and some basic points to remember. Some of these are:

1. *Concentration.* A player must have total concentration, especially in relationship to the ball, if his game is to be effective. By this we mean the player should be sure to watch the ball into the racquet and to keep the head

down in relationship to the ball, as one would in hitting a golf ball, rather than peeking up just at the moment the ball makes contact. This is a mistake that will result in not hitting the ball squarely with the power that would otherwise be gained if the eyes had been kept on the ball for that extra split second. Concentration on this skill contributes greatly to the success of a racquetball player.

2. *Grip.* In order to get power, direction, and placement on the ball, a player must have a tight, controlled grip on the racquet at the moment contact is made with the ball. A lot of beginning players hit the ball with a loose and wobbly racquet, therefore lacking the proper speed and power or direction and placement that they should have in making their different shots. It is imperative for a player to have total control of the racquet through a proper grip in order to execute the desired shot, and this requires proper grip.

3. *Hitting through the ball.* It is a common tendency for beginning players as they make contact with the ball to pull back and away from their swing rather than continuing through the swing. Pulling back results in a loss of power and speed and probably inaccurate direction and placement. Hitting through the ball is a simple fundamental that requires concentration; stay with the swing in relationship to the ball in order to make the shot effective.

4. *Anticipation.* After completing the swing and follow-through on the ball, the player must move the feet in anticipation of where the opponent is going to return the ball. The player is then in the best possible position to hit the ball again in turn. Racquetball is a game that requires movement and at no time does it allow a player to stand; rather, the player must hit and move constantly in anticipation of where the ball is going to be returned.

The player who will go back and review these basic fundamentals and skills and try to keep these things in mind during play will find that proficiency and skill will improve immensely. These people will become better players faster and will enjoy the game of racquetball to a greater extent.

basic shots
3

All of the basic shots in racquetball can be executed by using the forehand stroke, the backhand stroke, and, in some cases, even the overhead smash. It is important to practice these shots until a player has good placement and direction and the necessary power for each shot. These items will give a player overall proficiency and skill. After this has been accomplished, the player can utilize these shots with certain variations and combinations by using side-walls, front wall, and ceiling in order to gain the advantage over his opponent. (In the accompanying figures within this chapter, the opponent is assumed to be in some part of the shaded area.)

KILL SHOT

This shot is probably the most effective one. It is a shot that is utilized to terminate play, as the ball comes off the front wall so low and fast that it is impossible to return.

In order to execute a good kill shot, the ball should be hit from a low position off the floor. Any ball hit above the waist will be difficult to place in a kill position off the front wall. Also, it is important that the player have enough time to get into the proper stroking position in order to put plenty of force into the shot. Many beginning players attempt to kill too many balls. Proper court position will be the determining factor in whether to use a kill shot.

Front Wall Kill (Fig. 3.1)

This shot is hit directly to the front wall in a straight line and rebounds in a straight line. This is the most-used kill shot, as it can be hit along either sidewall.

With your opponent in a court area to the left of center, you intend to hit a Sidewall-Frontwall Kill. To which wall should you direct your hit and why?

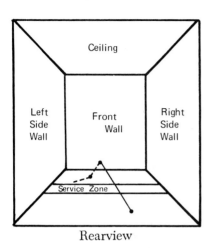

Fig. 3.1 Front wall kill

Ceiling

Left Side Wall

Front Wall

Right Side Wall

Service Zone

Rearview

Sidewall—Front Wall Kill (Fig. 3.2)

This shot strikes the sidewall and then the front wall so that the rebound of the ball is away from the opponent. The amount of angle on the shot is determined by where the ball is hit on the sidewall. As in all kill shots, one should hit the ball hard and low.

Front Wall—Sidewall Kill (Fig. 3.3)

This is not as effective as the other kill shots because the ball has a higher bounce from hitting the sidewall. Also, the rebound will be toward the opponent, so the ball must be hit extremely low.

PASSING SHOT

This is the most frequently used shot in racquetball. It can be hit when a player is forced to swing faster than usual at the ball and when it is not possible to get into a set position. The basic principle behind this shot is to have the ball rebound from the front wall at such an angle that it will pass an opponent (fig. 3.4). The ball should be hit low enough so that it will not reach the back wall and preferably it should be hit at such an angle off the front wall that the ball will not hit either sidewall. If it hits the sidewall, the shot loses power and gives the opponent time to recover and return the ball.

The passing shot should be used whenever an opponent is out of position. This shot is especially effective when an opponent is in the frontcourt or near the front wall.

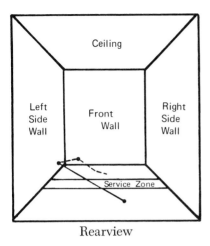

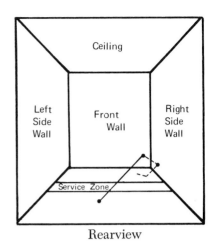

Fig. 3.2   Sidewall-front wall kill

Fig. 3.3   Front wall-sidewall kill

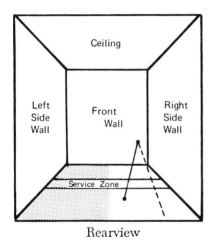

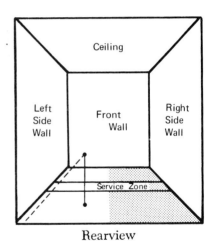

Fig. 3.4   Passing shots

Ceiling Shot (Fig. 3.5)

The ceiling shot is most effective whenever a player finds his opponent in the frontcourt position and wants to force him to move into the backcourt. The shot, if hit properly with the right amount of speed and direction, should force an opponent to retreat to the backcourt and to the back corner where the player will have difficulty making a strong return. The shot can be hit from anywhere on the court, but it ideally is used from the center and back-court areas.

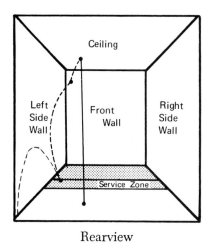 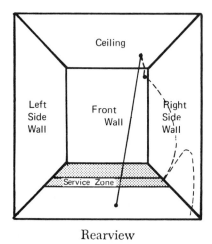

Rearview   Rearview

Fig. 3.5   Ceiling shots

The shot should be hit upward to contact the ceiling approximately three to six feet away from the front wall at such an angle that after hitting the ceiling, it will rebound sharply to the front wall and then rebound very high off the floor. With the proper rebound, the ball should come toward the back wall with a high arch, angling close to the sidewall and into the corner. The main objective is to get the ball to rebound with a high loft and a sharp drop to the corner or back wall.

In making the ceiling shot, the ball may be hit in more of a stand-up position, waist high or higher, and still be effective.

Lob Shot

The lob shot is similar to the ceiling shot except that the front wall is hit first. The ball is placed high on the front wall so that the rebound will come off close to the ceiling. Upon hitting the floor, the ball will rebound with a high arch and land close to the rear corner and back wall. It is important for a player to remember on this shot to keep the ball as close to the sidewall as possible. This will make a return difficult for an opponent.

The purpose of the shot, as in the ceiling shot, is to move the opponent into the backcourt and thereby gain position and advantage.

Dropshot

The dropshot can be used most effectively when an opponent is caught close to the back wall and deep in backcourt position. The shot should be hit to the front corners in such a way that it will drop sharply into the corners with very little rebound.

Do you know what type of shot is most used in racquetball? Where should your opponent be when you attempt the following shots: (a) dropshot, (b) forehand passing shot, and (c) ceiling shot?

The objective is to make an opponent run the full distance of the court in order to return a ball that has little rebound. It should be remembered that the shot must be hit firmly by the racquet, but that the swing is checked immediately after the impact, as there is very little follow-through. The shot can also be accomplished by using the overhead smash, but once again, the placement must be close or low to the front wall and into the corners.

Back Wall Play

One of the most effective and basic shots in handball relates to racquetball in practically the same way. This shot is probably harder to master than the normal forehand and backhand strokes, as it does require a turn to the back wall, pivoting to be in a position to hit the ball coming off the back wall. It requires great concentration in order to make a successful stroke on the ball. This shot is unusual in that the player will hit the ball with the flow that, if executed properly, can result in great power and low placement. The important thing to remember in making the back wall play is to position yourself properly for the shot so that you don't have to reach or run after the ball. It is imperative that you watch the ball closely during its flight to the back wall and as you make your turn toward the back wall in preparing for the shot. As you make the turn in the same direction that the ball is traveling, you must be prepared to immediately reverse your turn again and to pivot to the proper position facing the sidewall in order to make the forehand or backhand stroke. As you turn and pivot with the ball as it comes off the back wall, this will give you the necessary speed and power required to return the ball to the front wall with good placement. It is important as the ball comes off the rear wall that you position yourself far enough away from the wall and the ball to get a good swing at it and to allow the ball to drop to the desired knee-high position. As in your normal forehand or backhand stroke, you would start your backswing as soon as you start your pivot in relation to the ball and as the ball approaches you. You will step forward to the front wall with your lead foot and execute your forward swing, following through in the same manner as you would in hitting the normal shot. The important thing in this shot is to hit from a low position in order to make a solid and

Good timing is essential for speed and power in making a play off the back wall. Do you know when to start your backswing and which wall you should be facing at the end of the follow through?

powerful ground stroke. As you follow through with the completion of the stroke, your body will now be pulled around so that you are facing the front wall and moving your feet to get into the "ready" position.

MORE DIFFICULT SHOTS AND SERVES

After a player has mastered the basic shots he can now combine them into many shot combinations and variations. These possible shot combinations arise in a game due to the different court positions of an opponent. (In the figures accompanying this chapter, the opponent is assumed to be in some part of the shaded area.)

Soft Corner Dropshot (Fig. 3.6)

This shot can be directed to either the front wall or the sidewall with the idea of hitting the ball close to the corner. The shot can be used with the forehand and backhand strokes. It is also quite effective with the overhead smash. In using the soft corner dropshot, one must have good control of the ball and should not use a complete follow-through of the stroke. The ball is hit firmly, but much softer than a regular shot. This creates a short rebound or short drop on the front or sidewall toward the corner.

Sidewall—Front Wall—Corner Shot (Fig. 3.7)

This shot is most effective when the opponent is behind and to one side of a player. Until a player has completed a full swing on the ball, he must wait before he can move into recovery position. A greater angle off the sidewall will be used than in the corner dropshot.

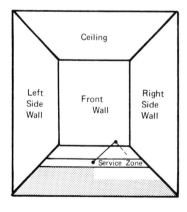

Rearview—Forehand   Rearview—Backhand

Fig. 3.6 Soft corner dropshot

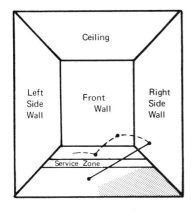
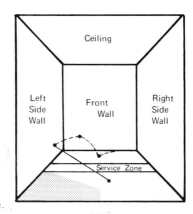

Rearview—Backhand   Rearview—Forehand

Fig. 3.7   Sidewall-front wall-corner shot

This shot should be hit with good power and low enough on the sidewall so that it will rebound from the sidewall to the front wall in a low flight and then come off the front wall with a low bounce. If this shot is to be effective, the ball should never hit the sidewall any distance above three feet; otherwise its rebound will angle off the front wall and will be high enough that the opponent will be able to reach it without any difficulty.

Crotch Serve (Fig. 3.8)

In executing the crotch serve, the ball is hit to the front wall about two to three feet to the side of center. The flight of the ball should come back over

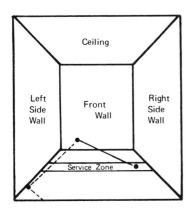

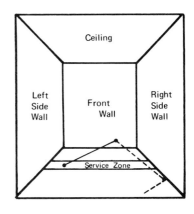

Rearview—Backhand   Rearview—Forehand

Fig. 3.8   Crotch serve

Can you successfully hit a diagonal serve to the forehand side 3 times out of 10? 5 out of 10? 7 out of 10? Can you do the same to the backhand side?

the front line and hit the junction of the sidewall and the floor at the same time. This must be a hard and fast shot. A good crotch serve will not rebound high enough to allow a good return.

Diagonal Serve (Fig. 3.9)

At times one may find the opponent playing towards the corner of the back-court in order to be in position to play an expected drive or lob serve. In order to keep the opponent honest, it is a good idea to change serves when this occurs. A serve that is effective against this strategy is the diagonal serve.

In executing this serve, the ball should be hit to the front wall approxi-mately three feet from the sidewall. The ball will then rebound from the

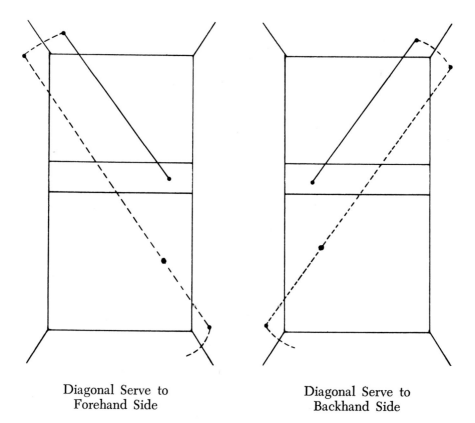

Diagonal Serve to
Forehand Side

Diagonal Serve to
Backhand Side

Fig. 3.9 Diagonal serve

front wall with good speed to the sidewall and will bounce into the back-court and then rebound into the back corner.

This serve can be used by hitting the ball to the front wall in two different ways. The first method is to hit the ball hard, fast, and low off the front wall, which causes the ball to come out of the back corner extremely fast. This makes it hard for an opponent to return the serve. In the second method, the ball can be hit much higher and slower off the front wall. This will cause the ball to have a more immediate and sharper drop into the back corner.

In either case, once the ball gets close to the back corner it will be extremely difficult for an opponent to adjust his defensive position.

Side Angle Serve (Fig. 3.10)

This serve is hit relatively low and quite hard. The ball should be hit to the front wall close to the center and approximately three to four feet from the floor; it will then rebound to the sidewall about three to four feet back of

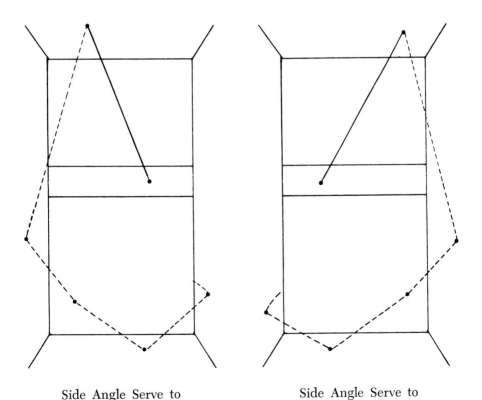

Side Angle Serve to
Forehand Side

Side Angle Serve to
Backhand Side

Fig. 3.10   Side angle serve

the short line. The ball will then come out from the sidewall very quickly and continue on back to the back wall diagonally toward the opposite corner where the ball will now bounce to the opposite sidewall. On the final rebound the ball will come off very close to this opposite sidewall and will drop to the floor close enough to the wall so that a return becomes quite difficult.

As a player becomes proficient in racquetball he will learn which shots to use in various situations. Once the shots have been mastered so accuracy of placement can be depended upon, one is ready to play top-level racquetball.

progress can be speeded up

4

In order to speed up progress in racquetball, one can engage in individual practice and general body conditioning. A person may have excellent shots, but if he doesn't have the strength and endurance to execute these shots over a period of time during a match, then his chances of winning will decrease. Not only will a player's ability as a racquetball player be improved by practice but also his general strength and cardiorespiratory endurance will be beneficially affected.

CONDITIONING

Racquetball requires a great deal of strength and endurance, especially in the legs. It is estimated that a player travels about 1.5 miles in an average racquetball game. Following are some recommended exercises for racquetball.

1. *Rope Jumping.* This develops leg strength and endurance and also increases the player's agility.
2. *Running.* A good combination to use in running exercises is jogging and wind sprints. A player should attempt to reach the point where he can jog for a mile, do wind sprints (run fifty yards, jog fifty yards) for a half-mile, and then jog a half-mile.
3. *Shuffle Exercise.* In this exercise the player assumes a position as shown in figure 2.2 (see page 17). The knees are flexed and the player shuffles in various directions as if playing in a racquetball game. A player should work to reach the point where this drill can be done for over ten minutes without stopping.
4. *Finger Push-Ups.* This exercise strengthens the muscles used in the various strokes.
5. *Finger Flip.* In this exercise, the player stands upright with his arms extended outward from the sides. He flips his fingers as fast and hard as he can for fifty times. Then he extends his arms over his head and repeats the exercise for fifty times. This is followed with the arms stretched in front of the chest; repeat again, fifty times. This strengthens the muscles

51

Effective practice is planned practice. Can you plan three individual practice sessions that include the specific techniques on which you plan to drill, the assumed location of the opponent during each stroke practiced and the level of success you hope to attain; e.g., 5 out of 10 good ceiling shots.

used in the majority of racquetball strokes, especially those muscles of the forearm.

6. *Sit-Ups.* This exercise is done in a supine position with the hands behind the neck and the knees in a flexed position. The feet are in contact with the floor, but not stabilized by hooking them under a weighted object. Flexing the trunk, the player then attempts to touch the chest to the thighs. If the resistance is too great it can be reduced by placing the arms alongside the body and doing sit-ups. This is an excellent exercise to develop the abdominal muscles.

7. *Body Control.* In order to become a good racquetball player, one must have control of his body. Quick starting and stopping, the ability to change direction, change of speed, and maneuvering form the foundation for successful racquetball.

The ability to control the center of gravity is a key factor in body control. A normal stance used in racquetball is one with the knees flexed and the feet comfortably spread.

A good drill to develop body control is to line up chairs in rows about six feet apart. The player then runs through these obstacles, varying his speed and direction. A variation using this same drill is to run toward a chair, fake to the left, and then run to the right.

There are many other exercises that a player can engage in to develop strength and endurance. If more information is desired it is recommended that a person obtain a book on conditioning or contact a reliable physical educator.

Individual Practice

It is important to remember that a person can learn bad habits as well as good habits. Too often the bad habits that one learns during practice come back to destroy the chance of winning during a match or tournament.

The objective that a person is trying to obtain through practice is to make the shots without a lot of conscious effort. In order to develop the nervous system pathways necessary for racquetball skills, the body must experience the basic movements many times. The basic fundamentals are the keys to becoming an outstanding player. Whenever a person goes into the practice court he should plan ahead what his practice is going to consist of. Just hitting shots at random, without a plan of attack, will not bring about the improvement that one desires.

In all of the individual practice sessions one should attempt to make the situation as similar to a game as possible. Many times players practice at half-speed and then find that all of this time was wasted when they try to adjust to an actual match situation.

Following are some individual drills that will be helpful in developing the basic skills necessary for racquetball.

The authors wish to express appreciation to Margaret Varner Bloss and Norman Bramall for the basic ideas utilized in these drills.

INDIVIDUAL DRILLS

Racquetball is a game in which a player can practice many of the shots individually without the help of a partner. The broken line (- - - - - -) on each drill indicates a setup. A setup places the ball in the correct location so that a specific shot can be practiced. The dot represents the contact point of the ball and racquet. The continuous line (————) is the desired direction and angle of the shot being practiced.

Wall Shot Drill (Fig. 4.1)

Setup   Toss the ball about head height onto the sidewall near the front wall and let it bounce to the floor.

Object   To stroke a forehand or backhand drive parallel to the side wall with control.

Hints   Note closely the angle the ball takes to and from the front wall. Begin with a short swing and gradually move back in the court as proficiency increases. Use both sides of the court.

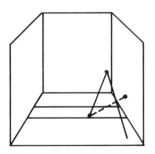

Fig. 4.1   Wall shot drill

Forecourt Wall Shot and Crosscourt Shot Drill (Fig. 4.2)

Setup   Hit the ball any place on the front wall.

Object   To play a wall shot or crosscourt shot from the area in the front court.

Hints   Note the height of the drive on the front wall, which is necessary in order to get correct length. Use both backhand and forehand strokes. Gradually move back as accuracy increases.

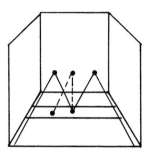

Fig. 4.2   Forecourt wall shot and crosscourt shot drill

Backcourt Wall Shot and Crosscourt Shot Drill (Fig. 4.3)

Setup   Serve the ball so it rebounds off the back wall.

Object   To play a wall shot or crosscourt drive from a defensive position in deep court.

Hints   To get depth, move towards the back wall and follow the ball as it goes to and from the back wall. Use both backhand and forehand strokes. Vary the drive with a lob.

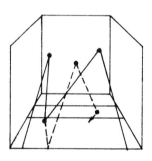

Fig. 4.3   Backcourt wall shot and crosscourt shot drill

Volley Drill (Fig. 4.4)

Setup   Toss the ball to yourself and forehand volley it to the front wall and then volley continuously.

Object   To increase reflex action. Begin by starting away from the front wall and gradually move closer to increase the tempo.

Hints   Volley with a straight forehand first, then a backhand. As skill increases, crosscourt the volleys. Vary positions toward the sidewalls to make the drill more gamelike.

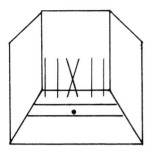

Fig. 4.4   Volley drill

Back Wall Drill

Setup   Serve the ball to the back wall. It may or may not hit the sidewall before the back wall.

Object   To learn the action of a ball rebounding off the back wall. As proficiency develops, vary the speed and direction of the setup.

Hints   Practice all of the shots on this type of setup.

Partner Drills

A great deal of improvement can be rapidly gained by working with another player. Repetition in hitting many specific types of shots will have a good carry-over to a game situation.

Serve and Return of Serve Drill (Fig. 4.5)

Description   Serve and repeat a particular serve until it is effective. A particular type of return should also be practiced. Notice that some serves force the receiver to make a certain type of return.

The two shots utilized most often in racquetball are the serve and the return of serve. They should be practiced until good skill is acquired.

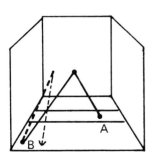

Fig. 4.5   Serve and return of serve drill

Can you and your partner stroke the ball crosscourt 10 times without missing? 15 times? 25 times? Can you do the same using both forehand and backhand strokes?

Crosscourt Shot Drill (Fig. 4.6)

Description   A and B are in position to warm up. These positions can be moved forward and back in order to crosscourt the ball repeatedly and to hit the opposite sidewall anywhere behind the service area. A partner should return the ball with a drive or volley before it hits the sidewall. Change positions with a partner in order to practice both the forehand and backhand.

Hints   Learn to play the ball at various heights on the front wall with varying amounts of speed.

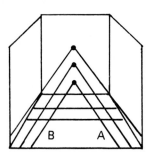

Fig. 4.6   Crosscourt shot drill

Crosscourt Drive and Crosscorner Drill (Fig. 4.7)
Description   A and B agree that one will crosscourt and the other will crosscorner. After a few minutes they may change shots and also change sides to practice the forehand and backhand of both shots.

Hints   Elevate the crosscourt drive. The other player then can volley the ball down the wall or crosscorner.

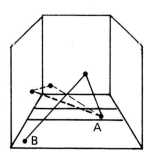

Fig. 4.7   Crosscourt drive and crosscorner drill

Ceiling Shot Drill

Setup   Hit the ball on the front wall so that it rebounds into the back-court.

Object   To hit a ceiling shot from a defensive position in the playing court.

Hints   Hit the ceiling shot so that it is close to the sidewall and deep in the court without rebounding off the back wall. Emphasize control without swinging the racquet too hard. As you improve, attempt to hit the ceiling shots in a continuous drill.

Four-Stroke Drill

Description   This drill makes the practice gamelike. The effectiveness of the first three or four shots involved in a point should be analyzed.

Hints   The quality of the serve and the return of serve set the pattern the play will take. Shots breaking off the sidewall and into the center of the court allow an opponent to maintain the center position.

SUMMARY

Although drills are helpful in speeding up progress, the best way to become an excellent racquetball player is to play as often as possible. After each game attempt to analyze the quality of shots and how effective the strategy of play was. Much energy can be saved by combining physical effort with thinking.

Repeating a stroke correctly over and over will eventually allow you to feel comfortable with a specific racquetball shot, but it is far different to practice shots than it is to hit the same shot under the stress, fatigue, and quick movements that are found in actual match situations.

patterns of play
5

It is now time to bring together all the information about the racquetball strokes and use it as a basis to play a match.

Many beginning racquetball players have the false assumption that the best way to beat their opponent is to hit the ball as hard as possible. In order to become a proficient player one must know court position and specific patterns of play. This chapter will cover singles, doubles, and cutthroat games.

COURT POSITION

It may be that the single most important factor in being a good racquetball player is court positioning. By being in the proper court position, you will be able to carry out your game plan, be ready to kill or return your opponent's shots, eliminate unnecessary steps and thus reduce the chance of early fatigue in the match, and be in an offensive position that will allow you to control the game and thus hit a higher percentage of winning shots.

The proper court position depends on the situation, but in most cases, a player should attempt to maintain a position on the playing court referred to as the center court area. This area extends from just behind the back service line to about 9 feet from the back wall and to within 2 to 3 feet of both sidewalls. Figure 5.1 contains a presentation of the center court area.

One of the chief reasons for controlling this center court area is that any ball hit with a sufficient amount of velocity to strike a sidewall, either on the way to or returning from the front wall, will angle toward the middle of the court. It will require a perfect kill shot or an unreachable pass shot to keep you from making contact with most of your opponent's return shots.

By learning to play in this court area, you will always be only one or two steps away from the majority of every ball your opponent can hit. The biggest mistake most beginners make is to play too close to the front wall, and thus find themselves in a poor court position.

You will want to start to think of the center court area as your home base. After nearly every shot, force yourself to return to this area. A good

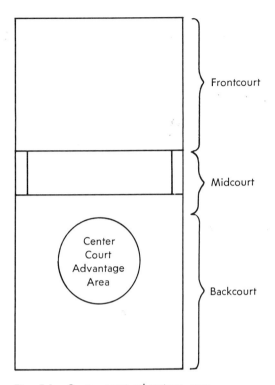

Fig. 5.1   Center court advantage area

method to practice this style of play is to find a friend who will play a match with you. Then tape an X directly in the middle of the center court area. This will give you a visual reference point to check as you play the game.

It should be pointed out that control of center court is being sought by both you and your opponent. Both players are usually in that area, jockeying for court position with the shots they hit. Therefore, your ability to hit the fundamental shots will also determine your ability to control the center court area.

You want to keep yourself in center court position, but you want to keep the shots hit to your opponent out of center court.

SINGLES STRATEGY

Server (Fig. 5.2)

When serving in singles, the rule states that the server must be within the confines of the service zone. In most cases, it is recommended that the server stand at the center of the service zone. This allows the best angles to both back corners and provides you with the most options of the places you might wish to serve the ball.

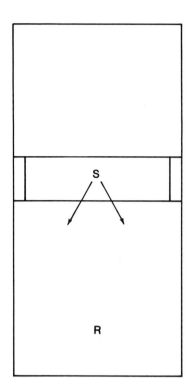

Fig. 5.2   Single serving and receiving positions

After completing the serve and after most shots, you should move immediately to the center court area. Have you made this return to home base
an automatic action? Try keeping a mental record for each 10 strokes of
the number of times you succeed in reaching home base.

After the server has completed the serve, the player should take a couple
of steps behind the short line. By doing this, you will be moving into a position that will enable you to control the center court area.

If you've served to the left, you would step behind the short line and
approximately one step toward the left wall. If the serve is to the right, then
move behind the short line and one step toward the right wall. See figure 5.2
for an example of these positions.

As you move to these positions, angle your body so that you can watch
your opponent. For example, if you have served into the left back corner,
your feet would be pointing toward the left front corner. A slight turn of the
head will now allow you to observe your opponent set up and begin to swing
for the return shot. This will allow you to anticipate and be able to react
rapidly for your return shot. A player who faces straight toward the front
wall will usually be caught flat-footed and in poor position for the return.

In serving there are two body levels to serve from. These are known as
the low zone and the high zone. The low zone is where the server contacts

the ball from a height approximately between the mid-calf and the knee. This level includes the drive serves and the low Z-serves. The attempt is to use a serve that will elicit a weak service return that can be put away by the server. If there is a problem serving from this zone, it is the difficulty of accuracy and thus a serve may rebound off the back wall for an easy return.

The high zone is the body area that is mid-thigh to chest high. The type of serves used in this zone are the lob serve and the high Z-serves. The attempt of serves in this zone is to put the ball into play without making an error on the serve. Serves from this zone usually do not elicit a weak return, so there is a longer rally before a point is won.

A player should be aware of an opponent's weakness in regards to the serve and use the shots that are most strategically sound. Changing the type of serve during the course of play can lead to confusion within the mind of the receiver, and thus keep the receiver in a defensive court position.

Most racquetball players are most successful when they put the ball in play by serving to their opponent's backhand.

As stated previously, the drive serve is the most effective serve. The ball should come off the left center side of the front wall so that the rebound will come back fast and low, clearing the short line while in flight and coming as close as possible and parallel to the left sideline, so that the opponent does not have an opportunity to get an open shot at the serve.

After the server has completed the serve, remember that it is important not to just stand. The rule states that the server must stay within the service zone until the served ball has passed over the short line. Immediately after this, the server should be stepping back of the short line to establish a playing position that will enable the server to have control of center court.

Receiver (Fig. 5.2)

As with the serve, the important factor concerning the service return is center court positioning. The receiver's position in singles should be one that is in the center of the rear court and about 3 to 5 feet in front of the back wall. From this position, you'll be able to cover either side of the court and thus cut down the chance of being aced on the serve.

A player should at all times assume the ready position. The player's feet should be spread approximately shoulder width, parallel with each other. The knees are slightly bent so that the weight is shifted toward the balls of the feet. The body should be straight and the head up, watching the front court in order to see the flight of the ball as it comes off the front wall.

The goal of the receiver is to achieve the center court position controlled by the server. Since the receiver is located in the backcourt, the logical means of forcing the server to exchange court positions is by means of a defensive shot. To do this, the receiver might use a ceiling shot or pass shot to force the server to move out of the center court area. Then the receiver moves in and by switching positions, the receiver has gained the advantage. Figure 3.5, chapter 3, contains an explanation of how a ceiling shot along the left wall might be used against a drive serve to the left.

If the serve is from the low zone, what types of serves should the receiver anticipate?

Also, the receiver can anticipate the type of serve that might be expected by observing the body zone the server uses to make contact with the ball. If the ball is hit in the low zone, then anticipate and prepare for a low drive serve or a low Z-serve.

If the ball is hit in the high zone, then the receiver can move up and take the ball on the fly before it hits the floor. Anytime you can hit the ball on the fly, you won't always have to hit a perfect passing shot or kill shot, as the server will still be standing in the service zone and in many cases the ball will be past the server before he can react.

It is important to remember to hit the ball away from your opponent and make them move wherever possible. It is much more difficult to hit a ball when in motion.

Rallying

As has been emphasized before, you will want to keep yourself in center court position and you will want to keep your shots out of center court. A shot that passes through the center court area gives your opponent the best opportunity to hit the ball without having to run for the ball in order to make contact.

A key point is to hit the ball away from your opponent. As your ability to hit the ball with control increases, make yourself aware of where your opponent is during the rally and force your opponent to run the furthest possible distance to retrieve your shot. A common error made by many beginners in racquetball is to try to hit the ball too hard and thus hit the ball through their opponent. The key is to hit the ball around the opponent. Figure 5.3 contains an example of this type of strategy.

One helpful hint is to hit the ball crosscourt while rallying with an opponent. This type of shot will prevent the ball from going straight to the back wall and then rebounding into the center court area, allowing your opponent to make an easy return on your shot. By hitting the ball crosscourt, you can force your opponent out of the center court area and thus you can gain control of this area. Figure 5.4 explains how to utilize this tactic in playing racquetball.

On all shots where your opponent is behind you, one of the best shots to use is a kill shot down the wall. By hitting the ball down the wall, your opponent's view will be partially obstructed and even if you hit the ball high, the ball will carry to the back corner and thus force your opponent out of center court. In order to hit this shot, you should aim for a spot on the front wall that is about 5 feet from the sidewall. Even though you may hit some balls that still go through center court, you will still win many points

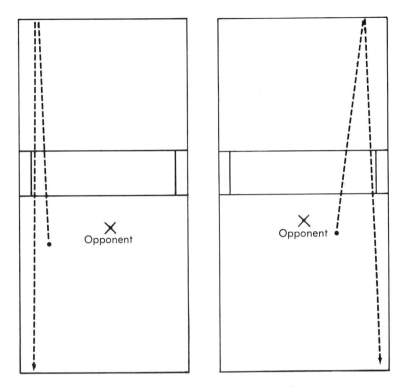

Fig. 5.3 Backhand down the line pass and forehand down the line pass

Can you give two general rules for placement of your shots.

because the added speed of the kill shot will make it more difficult to hit. Figure 5.5 contains a description of this type of playing strategy.

When you find yourself forced out of the center court area and in the backcourt, the two best shots to use are a passing shot or a ceiling shot. It is difficult to hit a kill shot from the backcourt unless you have spent considerable time practicing this shot. The passing shot is usually hit to the backhand, as this will probably be the weakest stroke of your opponent. The ceiling shot should be hit in such a manner as to force your opponent to run to hit the ball. In hitting the shots, it is important to try to hit a shot that does not strike the sidewall. After you have made your shot, you should always attempt to move to center court.

By combining the strategy of maintaining center court position and good shot selection, you should now be able to force your opponent to hit shots that you can take at the front and midcourt areas. This will allow you to be in control of the game and thus develop a winning racquetball style.

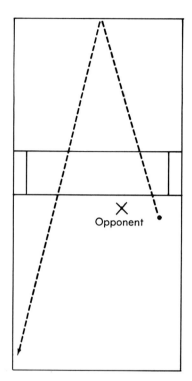
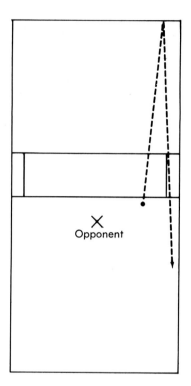

Fig. 5.4   Crosscourt shot away from the opponent

Fig. 5.5   Kill shot down the wall

DOUBLES

There are many excellent features to the game of doubles in racquetball. It is a good change of pace from the singles game, it allows you to combine a team aspect to racquetball, it is a means of having a coeducational type of game by playing mixed doubles, and it is less strenuous than singles, but still a very enjoyable experience.

Playing together as a unit is not too difficult if the two partners decide in advance what type of basic court position and strategy they will follow. A communication system should be used, so that one partner will call the shots during the rally so there are no questions as to which partner will return a given shot. An effective method to provide this information, concerning who is responsible for a shot return, is to use a simple "yours" or "mine." To reduce conflict and error during the course of play, it is best to designate one partner who will be responsible to call each ball throughout the match.

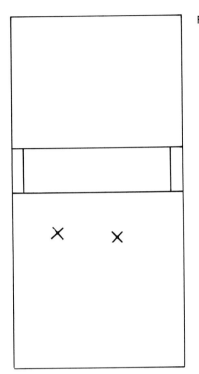

Fig. 5.6   Side-by-side formation

BASIC FORMATIONS

Side-by-Side (Fig. 5.6)

This is the most logical and efficient formation to use in playing doubles. In this formation, each player has the responsibility for one half of the court. If it is ever necessary for one player to get out of position, then the teammate shifts into the vacant area to cover the shot.

What advantage is gained when one partner is right handed and one is left handed? What disadvantage?

If a team is composed of one player who is right-handed and another player who is left-handed, then this allows the team to cover the passing lanes and serving areas with forehand shots. The possible weak area would be the decision to decide who will cover shots down the middle. If possible, the player with the strongest backhand should take these shots.

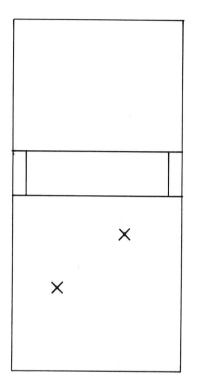

Fig. 5.7   Modified side-by-side formation

Modified Side-by-Side (Fig. 5.7)

Since most teams will be composed of two right-handed players, the modified side-by-side formation is a good style of play to use. The player with the best backhand will play the left side of the court and the right-side player has a major responsibility in covering the right front corner, as this is a potential area for scoring points.

The left-side player generally plays a little deeper to protect the backhand, and this sets up a diagonal formation for court coverage. By doing this, you are now utilizing the strengths of both partners.

I-Formation (Fig. 5.8)

The basic idea behind this formation is to have one player up and the other player back. This formation requires players with some special and unique playing skills. The front player has to be especially quick, very aggressive in covering the court, and have good skill in retreiving the ball. He or she also has to have the ability to hit good kill shots. The back player has to be skilled in hitting the ball from the deep court and has to be especially able to hit the ceiling shot with good control.

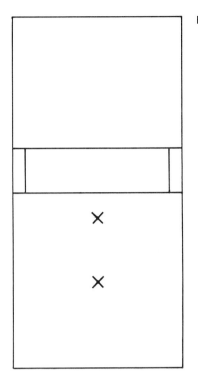

Fig. 5.8   I-Formation

The I-Formation for doubles play requires each partner to have special skills. What are the qualifications for the front player?

Center Court Strategy

As in singles, control of the center court area is a must to produce a winning game of doubles. By controlling the center court, your team is in the best position to return the majority of the opposing team's shots. Your team will be hitting shots that are closer to the front wall, and thus you will increase the chance of hitting a more accurate shot. It is also much easier to see the ball when your opponents are behind you and not partially blocking your view of the shot. And finally, since you usually don't have to hit a shot around another player, you have the opportunity to hit a wider variety of kill shots without the problem of hitting your opponent with the ball.

The serving team should use serves that will allow them to maintain a center court position, and the receiving team should always try to return the serve in such a way that the opposition will be forced away from the center court area.

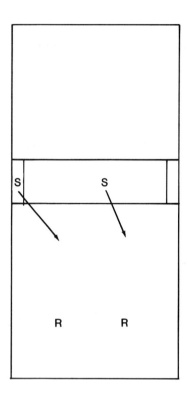

Fig. 5.9 Doubles serving and receiving positions

Serving (Fig. 5.9)

In doubles, the partner of the server must be within the confines of the server's box. The server is in the same basic position in the service zone as in singles. The server's partner must stay within the service box until the ball has hit the front wall and has come back and crossed the front line. After this has happened, both the server and the partner should move to control the center court area.

Proper serving is an important part of the doubles game. You should aim for the back corners the same as in singles. In doubles, though, accuracy is more important than power. A Z-serve to the weakest player is a good serve. A high lob serve that will cause a defensive return also works well in doubles. The thing to always keep in mind is to use a serve that will allow the serving team time to get into position to control the center court.

Receivers (Fig. 5.9)

The receiving team should try to return the serve using a shot so that the opposing team is forced out of the center court area, and then they should move as quickly as possible to gain control of this area for themselves.

If the serve is hit poorly, make an aggressive return by attempting a kill shot or drive it crosscourt. You may have to use a wider angle on the crosscourt shot so that you increase the chance of the ball going by your opponent. Attempt to have the ball hit the sidewall just behind the area of the court where your opponent is standing.

The volley shot, where you hit the serve before it bounces, can sometimes be used effectively against the lob serve. This will allow you to return the ball quicker and reduce the time that the serving team has to get to the center court area. The volley is not only a good shot against the serve but it is also a good shot to use in doubles, as it decreases the time your opponents have to react to your shot.

When in doubt as to the shot to use, either on the serve or during the course of play, go to the ceiling shot. This has excellent strategic value, as it may move your opponent out of center court position and gives your team time to jockey for an offensive position. Patience is an important part of the doubles game. Many teams are not successful because they are not willing to wait until the proper time arrives to hit the correct shot. By using a defensive ceiling shot, your opponents may make an error or hit a low percentage shot, which will allow your team to put the ball away.

The key to successful doubles, of course, is to play the other team's weaknesses. Doubles can be a great game, and by playing doubles, you can develop a wide variety of playing skills. You can then plan a strategy of playing the game that employs the combined assets of you and your partner to the best advantage.

Three Man or Cutthroat Strategy

In three man racquetball the rules to follow in court position are simple. When serving, try to attain the position as explained for the singles game. When receiving, then utilize the positions explained for the doubles game.

language of racquetball and the rules of the game

6

COMMON RACQUETBALL TERMS

Racquetball has developed in a short time into a game of national interest. Many of the terms and language used in racquetball are similar to those used in handball, tennis, and squash. In order to understand and communicate with other racquetball players the following list of terms are considered important.

Ace. A serve untouched by the receiver.

Advantage position. The position on the court where a player can hit most shots and control the game. It is approximately five feet back of the short line in the middle of the court.

Backcourt. The area back of the short line.

Backhand. Hitting the ball from the nondominant side.

Backswing. Taking the racquet back in preparation for beginning the swing.

Blocking. Preventing the opponent from hitting the ball by moving some part of the body between the opponent and the ball.

Court. The playing area.

Crotch ball. A ball hitting at the juncture of the service wall and the ceiling, floor, or sidewall or in the corners.

Cutthroat. A game involving three players with each player playing against the other two.

Dead ball. A ball that is no longer in play.

Defensive player. The receiver.

Doubles. Two players playing against two other players.

Drive. Hitting the ball hard to the front wall so that it rebounds on a relatively straight line.

Error. Failure to successfully return a ball during play.

Fault. An infraction of the service rule.

Follow-through. The continuation of the swing of the racquet after the ball has been hit.

Foot fault. Illegal position of the server's feet on the serve.

Forehand. Hitting the ball from the dominant side.

Frontcourt. The court area in front of the service line.

Game. The winning of twenty-one points, constituting a game.

Half volley. Hitting the ball just after it bounces from the playing surface.

Handout. A loss of serve.

Hinder. Unintentional interference with an opponent during play, resulting in replay of point.

Illegal server. Failure to serve the ball in accordance with the playing rules.

Kill. A ball hit so low to the front wall that it is practically unplayable.

Lob. A ball hit high and gently to the front wall, which rebounds in a high arc to the back wall.

Match. The winning of two out of three games.

Offensive player. The server.

Pass. A ball hit to the side and out of the reach of an opponent.

Placement. A shot hit to the spot where it was intended, which cannot be returned.

Rally. The playing time between the serve and the end of the point.

Receiver. The receiver of the serve.

Rest period. Intervals during and between games in accordance with the rules.

Screen. Interference with opponent's vision in attempting to play the ball.

Screen ball. A served ball that passes so close to the server that the receiver's view of the ball is obstructed; this ball should be replayed.

Server. The player hitting the ball to the front wall to begin the play of the point.

Serve-out. A player losing the serve in accordance with the rules.

Service box. In doubles, the area in which the server's partner must remain until the serve has passed the short line.

Service line. In four-wall racquetball, a line parallel to and five feet in front of the short line. In one-wall racquetball it is a line parallel to and nine feet back of the short line.

Service Zone. The area between and including the service line and the short line.

Shadow-serve. A served ball passing so close to the server's body on the rebound that the receiver is unable to pick up the flight of the ball.

Short. A serve failing to rebound past the short line.

Short line. In four-wall racquetball, a line midway between and parallel with the front and back walls. In one-wall racquetball, a line parallel to and sixteen feet from the front wall.

Sidelines. The lines marking left- and right-hand boundaries of the court in one-wall and three-wall racquetball.

Side out. Loss of service by player in singles or both players in doubles.

Straddle ball. A ball going between the legs of a player.

Volley. Playing the ball in the air before it has bounced.

RULES OF THE GAME

The rules governing racquetball are simple and easy to learn. A complete copy of the official rules can be obtained from the United States Racquetball Asso-

---

Do you know the service rules? Who serves first in the third game? How many serve-outs are allowed the first side to serve in a doubles game? Must serves be alternated to the opponents in doubles?

---

ciation, 4101 Dempster Street, Skokie, Illinois 60076. Following are resumes of the rules, which cover four-wall, three-wall, and one-wall racquetball.

The Game

1. *Players.* Racquetball may be played by two players (singles), three players (cutthroat), or four players (doubles).
2. *Description.* The game is played with a racquet and a ball in a four-wall, or three-wall court.
3. *Game score.* A game is won by the side first scoring twenty-one points. Points are scored only by the serving side when it serves an ace or wins a volley.
4. *Match score.* A match consists of the best two out of three games.

Serving Regulations

1. *Serve.* The serve shall be determined by a toss of a coin. In informal play contestants can rebound the ball from the front wall with the player landing closest to the short line winning the serve. The server of the first game also serves first in the third game, if any. Prior to each serve the server calls the score, giving the server's score first.
2. *Position of server.* The server may serve from anywhere in the service zone with no part of either foot extending beyond either line of the service zone. The server must start and remain in the service zone until the served ball has passed the short line. Stepping on the line is allowed.
3. *Violation.* A violation of the serve is called a fault and is an illegal serve. Two illegal serves in succession result in a serve-out.
4. *Method of serving.* The ball must be dropped to the floor within the service zone and struck with the racquet on the first bounce, hitting the front wall first and on the rebound hitting the floor back of the short line, either with or without touching one sidewall. The server shall not serve until his opponent is ready.
5. *Service in doubles.* In doubles the side starting each game is allowed only one serve-out. Thereafter, in that game, both players on each side are permitted to serve until a serve-out occurs. The service order established at the beginning of each game must be followed throughout the game. Servers do not have to alternate serves to their opponents. Serving out of order or the same player serving both serves is a serve-out.
6. *Partner's position (four-wall).* During the serve, the server's partner is required to stand erect within the service box with his back to the sidewall and both feet on the floor until the ball passes the short line. Failure to take this position during a serve is a foot fault.

7. *Partner's position (one- and three-wall).* During the serve, the server's partner is required to stand outside the sideline between the short line and back line until the ball passes the short line. Failure to take this position during a serve is a foot fault. If the server's partner enters the playing area between the sidelines before the served ball passes him, it is a fault.

8. *Dead ball serves.* A dead ball serve results in no penalty and the server is given another serve. They do not cancel any previous illegal serve and occur when an otherwise legal serve:
    a. hits the server's partner on the fly on the rebound from the front wall while the server's partner is in the service box.
    b. passes too close to the server or the server's partner and obstructs the view of the returning side. This is called a screen ball. Any serve passing behind the server's partner and the sidewall is automatically a screen ball.
    c. hits any part of the court that under local rules is recognized as a court hinder. This must have been agreed upon before the start of the match.

9. The following serves are faults and any two in succession result in a handout.
    a. *Foot faults* are the result of the server leaving the service zone before the served ball passes the short line or the server's partner leaving the service box before the served ball passes the short line.
    b. *Short serve* is any served ball that hits the front wall and on the rebound hits the floor in front of the back edge of the short line, either with or without touching one sidewall.
    c. *Two-side serve* is any ball served that first hits the front wall and on the rebound hits two sidewalls on the fly.
    d. *Ceiling serve* is any served ball that touches the ceiling after hitting the front wall either with or without touching one sidewall.
    e. *Long serve* is any served ball that first hits the front wall and rebounds to the back wall before touching the floor.
    f. *Out-of-court serve* is any ball going out of the court on the serve.

10. *Out serves.* Any of the following serves results in a handout.
    a. *Bounces* means the player cannot bounce the ball more than three times while in the service zone before striking the ball. A bounce is a drop or throw to the floor, followed by a catch. The ball may not be bounced anywhere but on the floor within the service zone. Accidental dropping of the ball counts as one bounce.
    b. *Missed ball* is any attempt to strike the ball on the first bounce that results in a total miss or in touching any part of the server's body other than the racquet.
    c. *Nonfront serve* is any served ball that strikes the server's partner or the ceiling, floor, or sidewall before striking the front wall.
    d. *Touched serve* is any served ball that on the rebound from the front wall touches the server or touches the server's partner while any part of the player's body is out of the service box or if the server's partner intentionally catches the served ball on the fly.

What should the referee call if the server attempts to strike the ball on the first bounce but misses it completely?

    e. *Out-of-order serve* is when either partner in doubles serves out of order.

    f. *Crotch serve* occurs if the served ball hits the crotch in the front wall and is considered the same as hitting the floor and is an out. A serve that hits the crotch in the back wall is good and is in play.

11. *Changes of serve.* A server is entitled to continue serving until:

    a. there is an out serve.

    b. two fault serves are made in succession.

    c. the server hits his partner with an attempted return before the ball touches the floor the second time.

    d. the server or partner fails to keep the ball in play by returning it as required.

    e. the server or partner commits an avoidable hinder.

Unusual Circumstances

    a. During the game and particularly on service every effort should be made to keep the ball dry. Deliberately wetting the ball shall result in an out.

    b. If there is any suspicion that a ball has broken on the serve or during a volley, play shall continue until the end of the volley. Upon inspection if it is decided that the ball is broken or otherwise defective, a new ball shall be put into play and the point replayed.

    c. Play will be stopped if a player loses a shoe or other equipment or if foreign objects enter the court or if any other outside interference occurs. If a player loses control of the racquet, time should be called after the point has been decided, provided the racquet does not strike an opponent or interfere with ensuing play.

Playing Regulations

1. *Return of service* (four-wall)

    a. The receiver(s) must remain at least five feet back of the short line until the ball is struck by the server.

    b. A legally served ball must be returned on the fly or after the first bounce to the front wall either directly or after touching the sidewall(s), ceiling, or back wall. A return touching the front wall and floor simultaneously is not a good return.

    c. In returning a service on the fly, no part of the receiver's body may cross the short line before making the return.

    d. Failure to legally return the service results in a point for the server.

2. *Playing the ball.* A legal return of service or of an opponent's shot is called a volley. The following rules must be observed. Failure to do so results in a serve-out or point.

Do you know the meaning of these racquetball terms: avoidable hinder, cutthroat, pass, screen, and straddleball?

a. The ball must be hit with the racquet in one or both hands. The safety thong must be around the wrist at all times. Only the racquet head can strike the ball. Switching hands to hit a ball is an out.

b. Hitting the ball with the arm, hand, or any part of the body is prohibited.

c. In attempting a return, the ball may be touched only once. If a player swings at the ball but misses it, he or his partner in doubles may make a further attempt to return it until it touches the floor a second time.

d. In doubles both partners may swing at and simultaneously strike a ball.

e. Any ball struck at in play which is returned to the front wall and then on the rebound or on the first bounce goes out of court is a dead ball.

f. Any ball not returned to the front wall, but which goes off a player's racquet into the gallery or into any opening in a sidewall, either with or without touching the ceiling, sidewall, or backwall, shall be an out or point against the players failing to make the return.

3. *Dead ball hinders (point replayed).* It is a hinder if a player unintentionally interferes with an opponent, preventing him from having a fair opportunity to hit the ball. Each player must get out of the opponent's way immediately after he has struck the ball and

a. must give the opponent a fair opportunity to get to and/or strike at the ball. If a player in attempting to get into position goes in the wrong direction and the opponent stands still, this does not constitute a hinder.

b. must give the opponent a fair view of the ball provided, however, interference with the opponent's vision in following the flight of the ball is not a hinder.

c. must allow the opponent an opportunity to play the ball from any part of the court.

d. must allow the opponent to play the ball to any part of the front wall and to either sidewall or the back wall in three- and four-wall courts.

e. must avoid unnecessary interference with an opponent or unnecessary crowding, even though the opposing player is not actually prevented from reaching or striking the ball, as it is a hinder.

4. *Other hinders*

a. A returned ball striking an opponent on the fly on its return to the front wall.

b. Hitting any part of the court that under local rules is a dead ball.

c. A ball rebounding from the front wall on the serve so close to the body of the server that the opponent is interfered with or prevented from seeing the ball. (Called a shadow ball.)

d.   A ball going between the legs of a player on the side that just returned the ball so that the opponent does not have a fair chance to see or return the ball. (Called a straddle ball.)

e.   Body contact with an opponent that interferes with his seeing or returning the ball.

f.   Any other unintentional interference that prevents an opponent from seeing or returning the ball.

g.   It is not a hinder when a player hinders his partner.

h.   A player is not entitled to a hinder unless the interference occurred on the backswing and such a call must be made immediately.

5.   *Avoidable hinders* (serve-out or loss of point). An avoidable hinder results in an out or a point, depending upon whether the offender was serving or receiving. The following are classified as avoidable hinders:

a.   *Failure to move* occurs when a player does not move sufficiently to allow an opponent to hit the ball.

b.   *Blocking* is when a player moves into a position effecting a block on the opponent about to return the ball or, in doubles, one partner moves in front of an opponent as his partner is returning the ball.

c.   *Moving into ball* is caused when a player moves in the way and is struck by the ball just played by an opponent.

d.   *Pushing* is deliberately pushing or shoving an opponent during a volley.

6.   *Rest periods between volleys.* Deliberate delay exceeding ten seconds by the server or the receiver shall result in an out or point against the offender.

7.   *Rest periods between games.* A five-minute rest period is allowed between games one and two. A ten-minute rest period is allowed between the second and third game. Players may leave the court between games, but must be on the court and ready to play at the expiration of the rest period.

8.   *Continuity of play.* Play shall be continuous from the first serve of each game until the game is concluded, except that during a game each player in singles, or each side in doubles, either during serving or receiving may request a time-out not to exceed thirty seconds. No more than three time-outs per game shall be allowed each player, or team in doubles. Deliberate delay shall result in a point or side out against the offender.

9.   *Safety.* The safety thong must be around the wrist at all times. The racquet may not be switched from one hand to the other. Both hands may be used on the racquet together in striking the ball.

10.   *Injuries.* Play may be suspended for up to 15 minutes for any injury. If the injured player is unable to continue, the match is forfeited. If the match is resumed and must then be stopped again for the same player, the match is forfeited.

11. Prior to each serve the server should call the score, giving the server's score first.

12. Any games postponed by a referee shall be resumed with the same score as when postponed.

13. *One-wall and three-wall rules.* Basically the rules for one-wall, three-wall, and four-wall are the same with the following exception:
    a. *Three-wall serve*, a serve that goes beyond the sidewalls on the fly, is a point or side out. A serve that goes beyond the long line on the fly but within the sidewalls is the same as a short.

OFFICIATING

All tournament matches should be conducted with a referee and scorer whose duties are as follows:

Referee

1. Brief all players and officials on the rules and local playing regulations.
2. Check the playing area for suitability for play.
3. Check the playing equipment and uniform of players and approve of same.
4. Check availability of other necessary equipment, such as extra balls, towels, scorecards, and pencils.
5. Introduce players and toss coin for choice of serving or receiving.
6. Take position in center and above the back wall of the backcourt and signal start of game.
   Note: In a three-wall match, referee's position is at the side of the court near where the sidewall ends. In a one-wall match referee's position is on the side and toward the front of the court on an elevated platform.
7. During game decide on all questions that arise in accordance with the rules. The referee is responsible for the entire conduct of the game including:
   a. legality of the serve and its return.
   b. calling of unintentional hinders, intentional hinders, and faults.
   c. preventing any unnecessary delay during the match.
   d. announcing when a point is made or server is out.
   e. deciding on all questions in accordance with the rules and all questions not covered by the rules.
   f. forfeiting or postponing a match at his discretion.
8. Matches may be forfeited when:
   a. a player refuses to abide by the referee's decision.
   b. a player fails to appear for a scheduled contest within 15 minutes.
   c. a player is unable to continue play for physical reasons.

9. The decision of the referee is final.

10. Approve the final score after announcing the name of the winner of the match and the scores of all games played.

Scorer

1. Assist referee in prematch responsibilities.
2. Obtain necessary equipment for scoring match, including scorecard, pencils, extra balls, towels etc.
3. Assist the referee in any and all capacities at the referee's discretion.
4. Keep a record of the progress of the game as prescribed by the tournament committee.
5. Keep players and spectators informed on the progress of the game by announcing score after each exchange. The scorecard should then be given to the referee for his approval.

bibliography

BLOSS, MARGARET VARNER, and BRAMALL, NORMAN. *Squash Racquets.* Dubuque, Ia.: Wm. C. Brown Company Publishers, 1967.

GURNEY, WALDEN O. "A Paddleball Skills Test for College Men." Master's thesis, Brigham Young University, 1966.

KOZAR, A. J.; GRAMBEAU, R. J.; and RISKEY, E. N. *Beginning Paddleball.* Belmont, Calif.: Wadsworth Publishing Co., 1967.

MARCHANT, WILLIAM S. "Telemetered Cardiac Response to Participation in Selected Duel Sports Activities." Master's thesis, Brigham Young University, 1970.

MITCHELL, ELMER D., et al. *Sports for Recreation.* New York: The Ronald Press Co., 1952.

Official Racquetball Rules. The United States Racquetball Assoc., 4101 Dempster St., Skokie, Illinois.

YESSIS, MICHAEL. *Handball.* 3d ed. Dubuque, Ia.: Wm. C. Brown Company Publishers, 1977.

questions
and answers

TRUE OR FALSE

1. On a serve in doubles, your teammate is allowed to be anywhere on the court. (p. 72)
2. Cutthroat is played with three players. (pp. 2, 72)
3. Racquetball can never be played with more than three players. (pp. 2, 72)
4. A "short" is an infraction of the rules which involves a penalty, and has to do with irregular serves. (pp. 71, 73)
5. A crotch ball on the serve constitutes a loss of serve. (pp. 70, 74)
6. The foot may be used to return the ball. (p. 75)
7. The receiver must stand behind the short line while the ball is being served. (p. 74)
8. In doubles the server must serve from the service box. (p. 72)
9. A server may not step over the short line when serving. (p. 72)
10. When the serve is swung at and missed, and then lands long, it is considered a long. (p. 75)
11. A server may serve from anyplace in the service zone. (p. 72)
12. A dead ball is a ball hit with such force to "kill it" that it dies on the floor. (p. 73)
13. The official rules say you can play with any type racquet. (p. 3)
14. In playing racquetball, you use the same ball as in handball. (p. 5)
15. A served ball striking the front wall, then the ceiling, before striking the floor, is a fault. (p. 73)
16. The serve may strike the sidewalls before it strikes the front wall. (p. 72)
17. The server must alternate serves from side to side. (p. 72)
18. Players on the same team must take turns hitting the ball while in play. (pp. 68, 75)
19. When a player is hindered intentionally, it is an out. (p. 75)
20. A good backhand is not necessarily important to develop. (p. 21)
21. In racquetball, it is necessary to win by two points. (pp. 3, 72)

22. Your foot may be touching the short line on the serve. (p. 72)
23. In the first inning of a game of doubles, both team members of the first team serve the ball. (pp. 3, 72)
24. A served ball is okay if it hits behind the short line after going between the server's legs. (p. 76)
25. Two "longs" retire the server. (p. 73)
26. On the serve the ball is allowed to strike both the front and rear walls. (p. 73)
27. A short is when the server hits the ball against both the front and rear walls. (p. 73)
28. When playing doubles, both members of a team get one serve at all times. (pp. 3, 72)
29. Cutthroat is a game of three players where two are always against one. (pp. 2, 72)
30. A receiver must play the serve on the first bounce only. (p. 74)
31. When scoring, a score of 21 to 20 does not decide a game, since a game must be won by a difference of 2 points. (pp. 3, 72)
32. The ball can bounce more than once before it is served. (p. 72)
33. A short is where the ball fails to hit the back wall on a serve. (p. 73)
34. Points may be scored by either server or opposition. (p. 72)
35. Opposition may not play a "short." (p. 73)
36. A serve which strikes the back wall and is designated as long may be played at the discretion of the defensive players. (p. 73)
37. Tennis balls are the official balls used in tournament racquetball. (p. 5)
38. If the ball is struck by the handle of the racquet in returning the ball, it is counted as a dead ball. (p. 75)
39. On serving, the server can hit the ball before bouncing it off the floor. (p. 72)
40. In play, if a player makes an effort to get out of the way and there is a reasonable opportunity for the other player to get the ball, no hinder should be called. (p. 75)
41. In doubles, the partner of the server must remain in his service box area until the balls strike the front wall. (p. 72)
42. A player who feels his view of the ball was impaired by an opponent can call "hindrance" in the absence of an official. (p. 75)
43. The hand is considered to be part of the racquet and the returned ball is still good and within play when struck by this body member. (p. 75)
44. When one player has attained a score of 21 points, he has won the game whether or not the opponent is within one point. (p. 72)
45. After one short, service is lost. (p. 73)
46. Only two players can play racquetball at one time. (pp. 2, 72)
47. Server must stand in left-hand side of serving box only. (p. 72)
48. We grip the racquetball racquet in the Western forehand grip. (p. 18)
49. When the ball bounces back on a serve and hits the server, it is played over. (p. 73)
50. If the score is 21-20, the game ends. (p. 72)
51. If the ball hits the ceiling at any time it is an out. (p. 74)

52. The server as well as the receiver can score.   (p. 72)
53. An ace is a game won by more than 11 points.   (p. 70)
54. If on the serve the ball hit the server, it is a hinder and should be played over.
                                                                 (p. 73)
55. A kill is a serve that is so hard that your opponent cannot return it. (p. 71)
56. A three-wall serve is a legal serve.   (p. 73)
57. A receiver must accept all serves.   (p. 73)
58. The side which is not serving the ball can score a point.   (p. 72)
59. When a player is interfered with by his partner, it is not a hinder. (pp. 71, 75)
60. A hinder is any ball that can't be hit or returned.   (pp. 71, 75)
61. A ball swung at but missed may still be played on.   (p. 75)
62. As long as the ball does not bounce more than once on the floor, a receiver
    may use any object to propel the ball to the front wall.   (p. 75)
63. If a ball breaks during play the point is replayed.   (p. 74)

MULTIPLE CHOICE

1. The score should be called
   a. after both sides serve   c. never
   b. at the end of the game   d. before each serve   (p. 72)
2. On the serve the ball must
   a. be bounced first
   b. be thrown to opponent first
   c. hit the wall and pass the red line before bouncing
   d. be thrown at the corner   (p. 72)
3. A crotch ball is
   a. a ball hit that strikes the back wall and front wall successively
   b. a ball that strikes a player below the belt
   c. a ball that strikes a connection of a wall to another wall or the ceiling
      or floor
   d. a ball that hits the ceiling and then the wall   (p. 70)
4. A ball which is returned to the front wall and rebounds from the sidewall or
   front wall in such a manner that it is impossible to get is
   a. a dead ball   c. a hinder
   b. an ace   d. a kill   (p. 71)
5. If the server steps out of the service zone while in the act of serving, it will
   constitute
   a. a point for receiver   c. a fault
   b. a side out   d. a hinder   (p. 72)
6. If a player's partner is hit by a served ball while in the service box, it counts as
   a. a fault   c. a hinder
   b. a side out   d. a dead ball   (p. 73)
7. When a served ball hits the front wall and two sidewalls before striking the
   floor it constitutes
   a. a short   c. a foot fault
   b. a side out   d. a two-side serve   (p. 73)

8. A hinder is
   a. a hard serve
   b. a good player
   c. a service that completely eludes the receiver
   d. where the flight of the ball is interfered with   (pp. 71, 75)
9. In doubles, if a volley is swung at, hit, but its course not altered, and the other partner makes the return, the play is ruled
   a. fault   c. ace
   b. successful return   d. hinder   (p. 75)
10. The nonserving partner in doubles may be hit ____ times while standing in the service box during a serve, before serve is lost.
   a. 1   c. 3
   b. 2   d. as many times as he wants   (p. 73)
11. The choice for the right to serve shall be decided by
   a. seeing who can hit the front wall closest to the floor
   b. arm wrestling for the first serve
   c. the toss of a coin
   d. whoever wants to serve   (p. 72)
12. When the ball is served and hits the crotch of the wall it is
   a. replayed   c. a loss of serve
   b. a good serve if it isn't short d. a hinder   (pp. 47, 74)
13. Before each service, the server calls out
   a. his score
   b. his opponent's score
   c. both scores with his first
   d. both scores with his opponent's first   (p. 72)
14. Cutthroat is
   a. 3 people in court all against each other
   b. 5 in court
   c. 3 against 2
   d. play by yourself   (pp. 2, 72)
15. A served ball striking the server's partner while he is still in the box is
   a. a dead ball   c. a fault
   b. an out   d. a hinder   (p. 73)
16. If a server strikes himself with the ball, it is
   a. in play   c. reserved
   b. dead   d. a serve-out   (p. 73)
17. There are ____ points that must be scored in racquetball.
   a. 11   b. 15   c. 21   d. 18   (p. 72)
18. A _____ is a phase of play wherein there is accidental interference of, obstruction of the flight of the ball not involving penalty.
   a. hinder   c. kill
   b. out   d. short   (pp. 71, 75)
19. On the serve, the receiver may stand
   a. anywhere on the court
   b. behind the service line
   c. behind the short line
   d. in the service box with his back against the wall   (p. 74)

20. The line running parallel with the front wall and dividing the court in half is called the
    a. service line
    b. center line
    c. short line
    d. long line   (pp. 3, 4, 71)

21. An infraction of the rules which involves a penalty and has to do with irregular services is called
    a. an ace
    b. a short
    c. a fault
    d. a long   (p. 70)

22. If a ball hits the back wall before hitting the floor on a serve, it is
    a. a fault
    b. a dead ball
    c. a good serve
    d. a long serve   (p. 73)

23. The best thing for an opponent to remember is
    a. watch his opponent
    b. watch the wall
    c. watch the ball
    d. watch his opponent's feet   (p. 26)

24. Stepping over the service line or short line in the act of serving would be classified as
    a. a hinder
    b. a fault
    c. an ace
    d. a replay   (p. 72)

25. If the server fails to serve the ball legally, as specified by the rules, it
    a. is played over
    b. is a fault
    c. is a free ball
    d. is a hinder   (p. 70)

26. When serving, a ball that strikes the sidewall before hitting the front wall is termed a
    a. pass
    b. hinder
    c. serve-out
    d. dead ball   (p. 71)

27. When the ball is dropped on a serve, it must hit no more than
    a. once
    b. twice
    c. three times
    d. four times before it is served   (p. 72)

28. A serve
    a. must hit front wall first
    b. can hit right sidewall first
    c. can hit left sidewall first
    d. can hit floor or ceiling first   (p. 72)

29. A hinder is
    a. recorded as a point to the player hindered
    b. played over
    c. a loss of serve if opposition is hindered
    d. a point for offensive team   (p. 71)

30. In doubles, the server's partner may leave the side box
    a. when server strikes the ball
    b. after defensive player has returned the serve
    c. after serve has crossed the short line
    d. anytime he wishes after the serve has hit the front wall   (p. 72)

31. A serve which cannot be played by the defensive player is termed
    a. corner shot
    b. crotch ball
    c. smash
    d. ace   (p. 70)

32. A side out means
    a. sidewall struck first on the serve
    b. kill shot hit along sidewall
    c. both partners are retired from service
    d. all of above   (p. 71)

33. A server's partner must
    a. stand back of the short line
    b. stand within the service box
    c. stand in front of the short line until the ball passes the service line on each serve
    d. stand in left corner of court   (p. 72)
34. The best position to stand in is
    a. any comfortable position
    b. one side to the front favoring the forehand
    c. one side to the front favoring the backhand
    d. in a balanced position directly facing the front   (p. 16)
35. If the ball hits your hand, it is considered
    a. a dead ball   c. a legitimate play
    b. a fault   d. a hinder   (p. 75)
36. Under which circumstances must the play be repeated?
    a. an error   c. a fault
    b. a hinder   d. a kill   (p. 71)
37. How many walls can the ball hit before the front wall on a legal service?
    a. no wall   c. 2 walls
    b. 1 wall   d. 3 walls   (p. 72)
38. A "kill" is
    a. flagrant violations of rules
    b. a hinder which results in physical injury
    c. a returned ball which upon rebound totally eludes opponent
    d. a service which strikes the opponent on the fly   (p. 71)
39. A long is
    a. taking too long to hit the ball
    b. hitting the ceiling before front wall
    c. serve hitting back wall before ground
    d. serve hitting behind service zone   (p. 73)
40. How much space is between the service line and the short line?
    a. 4 feet   c. 5 feet
    b. 3 feet   d. 2 feet   (p. 4)
41. What is the term for a service that can't be returned?
    a. ace   c. dead ball
    b. crotch ball   d. smash   (p. 70)
42. When the ball goes between a player's legs it is a
    a. hinder   c. crotch ball
    b. pass   d. short   (p. 76)
43. When the ball approaches you on your right side, which foot do you pivot with?
    a. left foot
    b. right foot
    c. neither, you meet ball face on
    d. none of these   (p. 20)
44. The number of walls a ball can hit on a service before striking the front wall and still be legal is
    a. one   c. any number
    b. two   d. none   (p. 72)

COMPLETION

1. Explain procedure for forehand stroke. (p. 18)
2. Explain procedure for the backhand stroke. (p. 21)
3. After serving the ball in singles to what court position should you move? Explain why. (p. 58)
4. What is the basic court position in doubles when playing a side-by-side formation? (p. 65)
5. List the basic types of serves. (p. 27)
6. Explain the "cobra" wrist action so important in racquetball. (p. 16)
7. List three individual drills that can speed up progress in racquetball. (Chap. 4)

ANSWERS TO EVALUATION QUESTIONS

Page	Answer and Page Reference
7	For safe play keep racquet thong around wrist; wear good, well-fitting shoes and soft socks; protect your face; stay out of path of ball; be aware of opponents' position; concentrate on the play; warm up before play. (pp. 6, 7, 14, 15)
14	The onset of perspiration indicates that the body has warmed up. When profuse sweating stops and the heart rate slows to 100 beats or less per minute, the player has cooled down adequately. (p. 15)
27	No answer, skill question.
28	A fault would be called if the ball fails to strike the front wall first; if the ball strikes three walls; if it fails to pass the short line on the fly; or if the ball hits the ceiling or back wall after striking the front wall. (p. 28)
34	The lob serve is difficult to control and its long air time gives the opponent the possibility of meeting the ball on the fly for a strong return. (p. 34)
39	Pulling back reduces the force with which the ball is contacted and may also slightly change the angle of the racquet face, thus causing a change in direction of the hit. (p. 40)
41	Send the ball to the left wall so that the rebound will be away from the opponent. (p. 42)
45	The passing shot is most frequently used. For a dropshot the opponent should be deep in the backcourt; for a forehand passing shot he should be out of position, especially when near the front wall; for a ceiling shot he should be in the front court. (pp. 42, 43, 44)
45	Start the backswing as you start the pivot and end the follow through facing the front wall. (pp. 45, 46)
48	No answer. Skill question.
52	No answer, paper and pencil exercise.
56	No answer, skill question.
60	No answer, skill question.

Page	Answer and Page Reference
62	A drive serve or low Z-serve may be anticipated. (p. 62)
63	Hit away from your opponent's court position and play to his weakest strokes. (pp. 62, 63)
65	Passing lanes and serving areas can be covered with forehand shots but there may be confusion as to who should play shots down the middle of the court. (p. 65)
67	The front player must be quick, aggressive, a good retriever, and skillful at executing kill shots. (p. 66)
72	The first server in the first game serves first in the third game. Only one serve-out is allowed the first team to serve in the doubles game. Serves need not be alternated to the opponents in doubles. (p. 72)
74	The referee should call a handout. (p. 73)
75	See pages indicated for definitions. (pp. 76, 70, 71, 71, 71)

QUESTION ANSWER KEY

True or False

1. F	12. F	23. F	34. F	45. F	56. F
2. T	13. F	24. F	35. T	46. F	57. F
3. F	14. F	25. T	36. F	47. F	58. F
4. T	15. T	26. F	37. F	48. F	59. T
5. T	16. F	27. F	38. F	49. F	60. F
6. F	17. F	28. F	39. F	50. T	61. T
7. T	18. F	29. T	40. T	51. F	62. F
8. F	19. F	30. F	41. F	52. F	63. T
9. T	20. F	31. F	42. T	53. F	
10. T	21. F	32. F	43. F	54. F	
11. T	22. T	33. F	44. T	55. F	

Multiple Choice

1. d	9. a	17. c	25. b	33. b	41. a
2. a	10. d	18. a	26. c	34. d	42. a
3. c	11. c	19. c	27. a	35. b	43. a
4. d	12. b	20. c	28. a	36. b	44. d
5. b	13. c	21. c	29. b	37. a	
6. d	14. a	22. d	30. c	38. c	
7. d	15. a	23. c	31. d	39. c	
8. d	16. d	24. b	32. c	40. c	

Completion

1. a. Grip. Stand the edge of racquet frame on a table and shake hands with the handle so that the **V** formed by the thumb and index finger is directly on top of racquet handle.
   b. Stance. Left shoulder will point toward the front wall and the right shoulder toward the back wall. Weight on the balls of the feet and the knees slightly bent.

  c. Backswing. Draw arm back with the wrist fully cocked and the racquet at around head height. The arm is bent at approximately a 90-degree angle.

  d. Forward swing. Shift body weight from right to left, with the knees bent. As you stride into the ball, dip the hitting shoulder to help lower the racquet. The wrist remains in a cocked position and the arm is bent and tucked in close to the side of the body.

  e. Impact. Contact is made off from the front foot. Just before impact snap the wrist forward so that the racquet face is vertical and traveling in a straight line into the ball. Keep good visual contact with the ball and let the ball drop as low as possible before impact.

  f. Follow-through. As the wrist is snapped through the ball, the left arm moves out of the way to pull the body through the final part of stroke. Body remains low, with bent legs, until stroke is completed. Racquet continues up behind left side of the head. Return to ready position as soon as possible for the next shot.

2. a. Grip. Hand is placed on the racquet handle so that the **V** formed by the thumb and index finger is directly on top of the left diagonal of the handle.

  b. Stance. Right shoulder will point toward the front wall and the left shoulder toward the back wall. Weight on the balls of the feet and the knees slightly bent.

  c. Backswing. Pull racquet back, with the wrist cocked, and the racquet head up and in line with the forearm. Arm is bent at the elbow and the knees are bent, with the shoulders rotated, so that racquet is approximately head high.

  d. Forward swing. Step forward and shift weight to the front leg. Rotate shoulders and pivot hips into the shot, hitting arm starts to extend but racquet is still back with the wrist in a cocked position.

  e. Impact. Just before impact, the hitting arm is nearly extended and the wrist starts to snap as the shoulder pulls the racquet through the stroke. Contact with ball is made off the front foot and at the moment of impact the hitting arm is fully extended and the wrist snaps through the ball. Don't allow wrist to roll over at impact, and maintain good eye contact.

  f. Follow-through. Allow racquet to follow through to right side of body. Keep wrist firm and the racquet horizontal to give maximum direction to ball. Hitting shoulder is pulled through and play returns to ready position for next shot.

3. Move to area just behind the back service line that is about 9 feet from the back wall and to within 2 to 3 feet of both sidewalls. This allows you to control the center court area so that most shots hit by your opponent that strike a sidewall will angle toward this area and allow you to return the shot.

4. Each player has the responsibility for one half of the court and attempts to be in an area approximately 6 to 8 feet back of the short line and about 3 to 4 feet from the sidewall.

5. a. drive serve   c. lob serve
  b. garbage serve   d. Z-serve

6. The wrist is held in a cocked back position at the start of the stroke and at the moment of contact with the ball is snapped or uncocked in order to impart the maximum power on the ball.

7. a. wall shot drill
  b. crosscourt shot drill   d. volley drill
  c. backcourt wall shot drill   e. forecourt wall shot drill

index